A CRADLE
of HALOES

A CRADLE of HALOES

Sketches of a Childhood

Bernie Taupin

AURUM PRESS

To my mother and father
for the reason . . .
To Toni
for the belief . . .
And to Marty Robbins
for 'El Paso'.

First published 1988 by Aurum Press Ltd,
33 Museum Street, London WC1A 1LD

ISBN 1 85410 005 X

Typeset by Bookworm Typesetting, Manchester

Printed in Great Britain by
The Bath Press, Avon

Preface

So my childhood goes on the wind of the silence
of memories, trees and the true make-believe.
But childhood explodes, scattering all toys
and it smashes through walls with a beautiful noise.

My Childhood
Jacques Brel
translated by Eric Blau and Mort Schuman

A life can be long and productive, or short and ill-spent. Irony can leave a life brief but fulfilled, or interminably empty. Whichever way the dice fall, it is safe to assume no two lives are the same. In this instance it is a short life with an option for extension – I am in no position to bare the facts of a full-scale, no-holds-barred biography, as I am at an age where such a thing would be unnecessary, if not presumptuous.

I have long perceived childhood as a dying art and whenever possible have fought religiously to reinstate it, believing whole-heartedly that little today is left to the imagination. We live in a world motivated by modern thinking and contemporary values where the pace occasionally tramples the process of infancy. The cocoon in which we are allowed to reside momentarily before maturity has become brittle, cracking prematurely under peer pressure. However, I remain logical and can see the sense in moving on from the Dark Ages. Without development of the mind, man might still fear the flame, and for all arguments in favour of progress I have no rebuttal save a simple *'but if only . . .'*

The Fifties and Sixties have been chronicled to the point of saturation, leaving them like bleached whale-bones on a distant shore, picked clean of carrion and dried by the sun. Hordes of historians, warming to this subject, have overlooked a smaller world in their mad dash to the pulse of this period – a rural world of warm tranquil summers and wild winters, farmers and schoolboys, rich brown earth and long silent nights; a world of soft rolling hills and great grey open skies, and of tribal children forged on the anvil of imagination.

Tackling this subject with sensitivity and passion, the likes of Laurie Lee and Dirk Bogarde* are among those who have given us a cinematic glimpse of this world in pre-war England. But what of we of the post-war era? What of the child rising from the embers of reconstruction, who sat on the sidelines as the two decades following the war years heaved and stretched their boundaries before folding into history; we who remained in the villages and walked in the fields constructing entertainment with the implements at hand, and performed in a theatre of our own design scenes from a world to which we were denied access?

To these and their kind I humbly offer this simple life, hoping that a fragment within might stir some forgotten memory and set your recall adrift upon a once-sacred sea, a sea for ever calm and far from the shores of reality where each of us must make our way. Take that memory, linger with it, and, when sleep is hard to find, turn to your pillow and erase the years. Drift into a quilted Victorian world of porcelain dolls and hot buttered toast, where the smell of leather-bound books and cedar chests permeates the freshly laundered flannel of your old pyjamas. Conjure up the sound of rain playing rhythmically on a nursery window as leaping imps dance in the flames of an open fire. Remember Peter Pan is only sleeping, only waiting to be gently woken. So go ahead, don't be ashamed, don't be afraid to stop and say, *'but if only . . .'*

Bernie Taupin
Southern California
1988

---

* *Cider with Rosie*, Laurie Lee, Hogarth Press, 1959
  A Postillion Struck by Lightning, Dirk Bogarde, Chatto and Windus, 1977

One

The village was still with an almost reverent silence, a tranquillity broken only by the occasional combine as it rumbled along Church Lane trailing in its wake the sweet smell of harvest. September's seemingly endless days were coming to a close and I for one knew it all too well. As the afternoon waned I would drift from the tea table into the garden and lie for hours in contemplation, soaking up the natural characteristics of those glorious hours. Soon the lusty winds of winter would roll in across the Wolds and bury the clematis and marigolds in a thick blanket of snow, but in the meantime I was determined to take full advantage of what little time was left.

Aromatic clouds of wood smoke drifted through the hedgerows and up into the trees, mingling with the scent of the autumnal earth. The freshly mown lawn was a bed like no other, fragrant and soft, its coolness connecting comfortably with my skin through the thin cotton of my school shirt. To sprawl there with what Kenneth Grahame called 'long waking dreams of summer' was all I wished for; all else was secondary. Stretching into my tenth year, fantasy figured prominently in my life. It balanced itself unevenly with the real world, which took a back seat.

My world was a special one filled with adventure and romance. Literary heroes existed and secret places made themselves known to those who believed in the power of magic. This was not to say that I was a complete introvert who saw goblins and gremlins in every waking shadow. I was merely the product of a warm, compassionate family who introduced me at an early age to the wonder of books. This encouragement not only sowed the seeds of a vivid imagination but laid a deep-rooted groundwork for the distant future.

In the literary stakes, A. A. Milne's little bear was the first character to enter my life, at a time when I could barely comprehend life itself. The 'Hundred Acre Wood' was a home in my head and Pooh, Piglet and Tigger were familiar friends. Soon after this I was foraging into the riverbank world of *Wind in the Willows* or travelling to Narnia courtesy of C. S. Lewis. So many worlds unfolded as I, wide-eyed in wonderment, allowed them to engulf me. It was a simple time and the beauty of childhood hugged my soul and carried me on wings of fancy. Even then, with my back pressed against the cool earth and my eyes zeroed in on the heavens, those wings of fancy were transformed into the wonder of aeroplanes. Several decades later they have lost little of their fascination for me. A sense of expectancy and excitement still fills my heart each time those steely wheels fold beneath me and the roar of engines points me towards the clouds. Then, in my utopian ideology, those silver birds never landed at Gatwick or Cleveland. Not for them the drizzle-soaked runways of Glasgow and Buffalo – to this child those planes touched down only in the most romantic places. Their vapour trails could be followed to Marrakesh, Casablanca and Nepal. They would dive and swoop through the Carpathians, those vast sentinels of Romania, staring with bleak foreboding at the ghosts of Transylvania. They carried brave explorers, whose travels led them from Aztec ruins to crumbling Tibetan monasteries; men who pitted their wits against danger in Amazonian jungles and lost valleys, where there were 'little green-eyed idols to the south of Kathmandu' and 'She-who-must-be-obeyed'. All this and more rushed like a locomotive through my fertile mind as I rode square on the shoulders of H. Rider Haggard and Edgar Rice Burroughs.

The county of Lincolnshire, for all its efforts, will never win any prizes as one of England's fairest. Its bleak terrain has suffered the slings and arrows of a cruel wind since time immemorial. Born out of the North Sea, the winds whip through the fishing ports of Grimsby and Hull, out over the flat rich farmland. Considering its drawbacks, Lincolnshire does have something to offer in Roman history, numerous remains still being found buried beneath the arable soil. The Romans built strong walls and made many of the thoroughfares that cut through this, the second largest county in England. Now, some may say that a road's a road and a wall is, after all, only a wall, but these and other remnants of the past give Lincolnshire an appealing barbaric quality.

This was my birthplace and at the time I don't recall finding anything to complain about, for it was all I knew. So it was with a severe smack on the rear that my rudimentary squawk echoed across this savage land, from an isolated farm surrounded by kale and potato fields somewhere off the main road between Sleaford and Lincoln. It was spring and the hawthorne and honeysuckle were stirring from their winter retreat. New leaves formed as their dying predecessors crumbled and returned to the earth. Young saplings braced themselves against the season and lambs bleated in makeshift pens.

My earliest recollections are of crawling on a rag rug in front of the Aga as my mother busied herself with domestic chores. As we had no electricity, paraffin lamps and candles were dotted strategically around the house. There were tell-tale signs that although the war had ended several years earlier, matters were still in disarray – a ration book on the sideboard, a mildewed roll of stamps on a high shelf. Clinical-looking bottles of concentrated orange juice and tins of powdered milk were stacked in the corner of the washroom. To me it all resembled army surplus, but to my parents I'm sure it was a grim reminder. I was, of course, too young to comprehend, but things around me did take on a decidedly black and white hue, a sense of struggling to tidy up after a major disruption. Here was evidence that although the war was over, the scars had not yet healed.

Other than these brief reflections, my first years aboard the fast-changing face of planet Earth were relatively simple. My mother bore down on the handle of her mangle, my father tended his stock and my elder brother and I careered happily around the garden on our tricycles, oblivious to the readjustments of the turbulent Fifties.

Daily the rooks would scream in the elms and the seagulls swooped in the wake of the drills to pirate the fresh seed from the earth. After dark we lay in our beds and watched as great tree limbs illuminated by the moon brushed the window and cast wild shadows on the wall. Warm and secure, we fell asleep to the sound of the wind and the hoot of owls in the wood beyond the ditch.

> *In duffle coats and dirty socks*
> *The years had eyes in the sky that watched.*

I'm told that I didn't cry on my first day at school, something which I rather regret. I would have enjoyed it if my first brush with authority had been of a revolutionary nature. But it was without a fuss that I entered through the hallowed portals of St Joseph's Catholic School in Sleaford. I do not wish to dwell on this phase, as there is little I recall, except that I had a friend with enormous ears called Ronnie Dibble and that there was a kind old priest who sold coconut-ice every Easter. Unfortunately I hated coconut, but I did like him and that seemed a good compromise with the Lord. We were transported to and from school in a dilapidated old bus somewhat like the ones seen carrying Bolivian peasants in steamy jungle epics. Our driver was a congenial soul named Fred who made clambering aboard that juggernaut a pleasure, even at a time of day when dreams from the night before had barely cleared our heads.

We remained at the same school even after my father was relocated to a nearby village, and it was here that I first experienced culture shock. Had my father been party to the crime of the century? Had we been the benefactors of some deceased relative's wealth? All this and more ran through my head as we drove through the gates of Louden Manor. Here before us lay the most splendid sprawling country home. Surrounded by lush rose gardens and spinneys of fern and bracken, it dwarfed the neighbourhood with regal splendour. At the rear, a gravel drive circled several stables and a lush paddock, and farther on a thriving orchard bore crisp apples and juicy black plums. There was nothing whatsoever mysterious about this move; my father's employers had simply needed to sell our old farm and so had moved us into one of their other properties. Luckily it happened to be their finest and, in their wisdom, they furnished me with nirvana.

Summers at Louden were blissful. The manor had a distinct

4

magic, being the kind of place where secret passages held a wealth of treasures. Even the threat of each approaching school term could not deter my cravings for the adventure inspired by this wonderful old home. It permeated me from its very foundations right into the realm of my senses. I fought great battles, rode the high seas and generally made the world a better place in which to live.

It is not my intention to delve into the background of my family, for I would prefer them to remain humane shadows in the sketchbook of a simple childhood. However, in the case of John Leonard Patchett Cort, affectionately known to us as 'Poppy', I beg to make an exception. My maternal grandfather had an effect on my life so strong that I feel it cannot be ignored. Although he died when I was only nine years old, my memories of him remain with me as vividly as if it were yesterday. He was indeed the consummate gentleman in every sense of the word. Gaining his master's degree at Cambridge, he went on to tutor in the classics with an educational flair seldom found in the teaching profession. Distinguished, kind and wise, his intelligence shone like a diamond in the rough. He instilled in me new passions, a caring for the quality of words and the stimulation of verse. Both as a botanist and naturalist, his enthusiasm for flora and fauna was unbridled. The study at his home in Baslow was a veritable goldmine of information on both subjects. Along the walls hung cases of carefully mounted butterflies and moths, their many-splendoured wings reflecting the light as it fell through the open window.

Hand in hand we would scour the countryside in search of bugs and insects, and for each one apprehended Poppy would have some strange Latin name which, when repeated, rolled off my tongue as guttural gibberish. We had our special places, and none more special than the bridge that forded the stream in Priorholme Park. Of all places that pertain to my childhood, this remains the most memorable: a place where it seemed summer was for ever present and a warm sun always hung in a cloudless blue sky. Poppy and I would sit in the soft grass beside the cool clear stream and watch the world float by. Dragonflies hovered over a host of water-lilies as small green frogs watched with languid eyes. Turquoise kingfishers swooped into the water where pike and roach could be seen as if through glass. In the reeds and bulrushes along the bank mayflies glided lazily while, below them, voles and water-shrews scurried undercover away from human scrutiny.

Time seemed to stand still and it was almost possible to smell the silence. The sun's rays had a therapeutic quality that caressed and lulled us into a sense of well-being. On the bridge we played Poohsticks, a game devised by a well-known bear of very little brain. Like him and Piglet, Poppy and I would toss a twig apiece into the water one side, and watch them as they raced out the other. This simple form of entertainment kept us constantly amused and we never seemed to tire of hurling our vessels into the stream. Rushing to and fro, I squealed my encouragement, and although Poppy moved a little slower, at no time did his energy flag. Eventually I was always the one to run out of steam and would throw myself into the tall grass, exhausted.

Poppy's visits to Louden were always special and a pat on the head and a 'My, haven't the little men grown!' were standard procedures. The love in his eyes was genuine and the soft smile that broke from the corners of his mouth unforgettable. On the front lawn he would conduct family cricket matches and in the evening he would recite stirring narratives as we perched on his knees before the fire. I can still see him now, wrapped in his blue robe, climbing the stairs to bed where he would lie reading. On the table beside him sat a red tin containing his favourite chocolate digestives. Into this he would dip occasionally, savouring every bite as he absorbed the printed page. While my parents were always my guidance, this man was responsible for the hammer of appreciation that pounds in my heart whenever art brings tears to my eyes, or the word moves me and the song lifts me.

Some monuments time can never replace
To rebuild an age that will never be seen again.

The seasons dissolved into one another at a leisurely pace, each heralding the other with some familiar sign. It was during the time when the swallows were returning to the wire that we came to possess Sheba, a large smooth-haired sheepdog which my father had received as payment for some veterinary act. Being skilled in this area, he was often called on by locals to tend a sick animal or, on occasions, to do away with one. Sheba, although loving, was totally psychotic and completely unmanageable. From an early age she was banished to the confines of a converted chicken coop on the edge of the paddock. Howling like a banshee, she would strain at her chain until her eyes rolled back and her tongue sagged from the side of her mouth. Convinced that any living creature within sight was a potential friend, she was not satisfied until they had acknowledged her presence. Her eating habits were far from savoury, and anything placed between her paws was destined for the scrap heap residing down her digestive tract. Sheba soon outstayed her welcome and later met her Waterloo in the following manner.

My mother, desiring to cheer us up during an attack of mumps, thought it might be nice to bring Sheba to visit us in our sickbeds. With much coaxing she was enticed into the house, firmly affixed to the parental wrist. Aside from a little tug and pull, all went smoothly until they reached the incline of the stairs. This foreign obstacle was not something with which Sheba was familiar and, half-way up, she decided to have a fit. With a howl of despair, she made a dramatic ninety-degree turn and fled panic-stricken from whence she came. Unfortunately my mother, still attached to the hysterical hound, was dragged in a horizontal position on an unceremonious tour of the house. As dawn rose the next day there came with it an unusual and permanent silence from the vicinity of the chicken coop.

Several months later my mother was to be on the receiving end of yet another pet's outburst. This came in the form of a sleek black cat called Shampoo, whose rather superior attitude did not endear her to the family. It was summer and we had left this ungrateful feline in the care of a neighbour. My father, having some time off, had taken us to visit his family in the west of France. On our return we learned that Shampoo had not taken kindly to our desertion. Refusing to acknowledge her foster mother, she had ignored all advances and grown wild, taking up residence in the local graveyard. Attempting to return the cat to the fold, my mother tried with comforting words and a saucer of milk to console her. She reacted ungratefully to this kindness and, with a venomous hiss, attacked my mother's arm as if it were a wounded starling. This action sealed her fate, for it took several stitches and a series of shots to repair the hand of friendship. Later that night as we prepared for bed, a single shot was heard from the direction of the graveyard. Shampoo, it seemed, had chosen her permanent home.

> *. . . always pray there's a reason why*
> *a butterfly's born in a shroud.*

Disembarking from the school bus one evening, my brother and I looked up to see the beacon of change sprouting from our chimney. Television had come to our home and with it a new age of enlightenment for yours truly. Whooping like heathens with our hearts on fire, we tore across the open ground towards the house. Hastily we wiped our feet and shuffled into the living room. There on the sideboard it sat, its walnut case reflecting our anticipation. My father extended a cautious hand towards the control knob – merely switching it on seemed ritualistic. You may think all this is overdramatic, but bear in mind that up to this point the world for us had been a somewhat singular place. All that existed to entertain us was forged from our own imaginations, so the acquisition of this appliance was like the installation of a door to another world. The surreal and the real were bound closer together now, and things of which I had once been ignorant would be accepted and incorporated into my games.

Between 'Crackerjack' and 'Muffin', the day-by-day machinery of government and war rumbled through the tube. Even to an impressionable eight-year-old, words such as 'Suez' and 'Algeria' became commonplace. Not that I took the remotest interest in them, as they were merely strange words in a grim setting, accompanied by anxious faces and urgent speeches. 'Bang, bang' became the universal sound of death, not the playful utterance that sent my brother crashing to the ground unhurt when two fingers were pointed in his direction. Goodies and baddies were clearly defined by this box. Charles de Gaulle and the Lone Ranger lived in a twelve-inch frame, sharing the same time and space and, blended together, they put a hard edge on a fluid world. Television was a springboard, a part of growing up that I accepted readily as a product that dished drivel and dreams equally into our home.

Louden continued to be a textbook for my growth. It saw battle scars inflicted and healed without too many tears, each cut and bruise attended to by gentle hands. A leg savaged by nettles could be soothed by rubbing it with dock leaves, and anything plucked from bush or branch could be counted on to cure everything from hepatitis to haemorrhoids. Although I never suffered the sting of an angry wasp or bee, those around me would suffer frequently. For these wounds there were so many poultices in practice that if someone told you to 'pee on it', it would have seemed feasible. Jeans and trousers were attire of the future and our childhood was spent in shorts, our ruddy legs exposed to the elements. The sure sign of a sissy was a knee unscathed by scab or scar. Although I was the recipient of countless bites, bruises and splinters, I managed to survive. Illnesses were the rudimentary ones and mumps, measles or chicken pox were annual events. I also ran the gauntlet of coughs and sneezes that left me immobile, full of rosehip syrup and reeking of Vicks Vapour Rub.

It was during a bout of flu one winter that my mother began to hint that we might be leaving our Shangri-La. For me this marvellous old home was hunky dory and as long as we were free to dwell there, I cared little who owned it. It never occurred to me that my father might be yearning for his independence and for freedom from the will of others. All his life he had served someone, a valuable asset to whomever paid his wage, but now his time had come. The winter of his discontent had passed and, with the new spring, he was ready to move on. Pooling his resources, he took the brave step down from bonded security to smallholder of freedom. The future looked uncertain and leaned towards a radical change in comfort, but the outcome already shone like a light in my parents' eyes – the risk was worth the challenge and that was good enough for us.

When John Betjeman wrote 'Kirkby with Mickby-cum-Sparrowby-cum-Spinx is down a long lane in the county of Lincs', he was saluting the quaintly named villages of Lincolnshire. One he forgot, but would have found fitting, was Bramby-by-Huddle, an almost microscopic settlement by today's standards of growth and development. Bramby sits on a rise of ground east of the Ermine Street between Lincoln and Brigg. The surrounding area is a maze of sister villages all christened with equally bizarre names, many of them ending in the customary 'by', a tag indicating they were once settlements of the Danes.

Bramby appeared like Brigadoon before us. Immobile in the evening light, it welcomed us warmly, aware that we were pioneers in search of our destiny. Our property lay in the centre of the village and consisted of two decrepit houses sitting on a patch of uneven wasteland. In addition, there was what at first appeared to be an impressive three-acre field; on closer inspection this started out firmly, only to slope down eventually into a soggy quagmire. The only other buildings were a battery house and a dilapidated barn. This was to be the stepping-stone to our fortune, and the commodity upon which it was to be built was the chicken.

As the days proceeded Maltkiln Farm, as it was called, took shape. We set up residence in the larger of the two homes and left the other to a wizened old lady whom we had discovered still living there. Her senility and deafness had been a boon to her in dealing with anything resembling an eviction notice. Judging by the decor of her home and by her demeanour, it seemed that there had been a serious error on someone's part in failing to inform her of the advent of the twentieth century. Of course my father allowed her to stay, reasoning that her remaining time was limited. More resilient than we imagined, she hung on for some time with a horde of cats and a pantry resembling a laboratory. As for myself, I was quite convinced she was a fully paid-up member of the broomstick brigade, and I would gaze each night out of the window expecting to see her jettison herself from the chimney into the night sky.

Being the 'hail fellow well met' type, my brother infiltrated the local clique in no time at all. Several years my senior, he was decidedly more approachable than I and found it easier to fit into his surroundings. The shuffling brood to which he attached himself was a pleasant enough group and took to him immediately. Each one of the boys bore the characteristics of the archetypal farm lad, from muddy wellies to tousled mane. Their pink faces laced with freckles bobbed about beyond the garden wall, calling the roll and picking sides for soccer. As it happened, my brother's feet were quite proficient at this sport and his name was always on the list when they dibbed for team members. With baggy breeches flapping in the wind and the constant sniffling of runny noses, Taupin major and his cohorts skipped off to do battle, leaving Taupin minor to the comforts of his own imagination.

It would be some time before I would make any close friends, and aside from several acquaintances that never lasted long, I preferred to amuse myself alone. When the need for companionship arose, I simply invented a friend. A great deal better than the real thing, they didn't become argumentative or go home to tea at the most inconvenient times. They did not pummel, shove, giggle or do any of the other annoying things that best mates seemed to practise. For the most part my entertainment was conceived in this way until the dawn of my teens. From time to time during my chosen solitude there were amiable souls who drifted in and out, and one I should not fail to mention was a genteel giant called John Spaulding.

John's strong point for survival in my selective roster was that he would do absolutely anything I told him. I recall that he was very large and pink, and spoke like a baby, which made him the object of ridicule and abuse. All this he took in his stride with never the slightest hint of retaliation. This surprised me, for judging by his size he could have swatted his opponents flat like ticks on a bull's back had he cared to. He seemed to enjoy being part of my games and never complained when he was constantly killed by my lightning draw or lithe and deadly sword. He was the perfect sidekick, a pre-pubescent Gabby Hayes acting as Pancho or Tonto and doubling as Little John and Friar Tuck to my Robin Hood. He became a fixture, happily agreeing to my every whim until the inevitable wind of change came with the death of his tyrannical father. Released from bondage and no longer timid or scared of retribution, he grew from within the confines of his insecurity into a pleasant young man devoid of bitterness towards his early weaknesses.

While my father's able hands attended to the everyday delivery of eggs, my mother attempted to make a liveable domicile out of our spartan surroundings. In our seesaw system of house moves, once more we had achieved the lowest position. Maltkiln Farm was no Louden Manor; it was a dark, damp crumbling building which in all honesty should have had a stick of dynamite inserted in its foundations years before. The front terrace was so dilapidated and distorted by age that we referred to it lovingly as 'The Alamo'. The interior of this bohemian dwelling was cluttered

11

with odd furnishings vying for space in our limited quarters. Innumerable draughts dogged the devices built to repel their chill, while in the dead of night subterranean sounds emitted from the skirting. It was a cold home and more than a little uncomfortable, but for all its faults my mother managed to tap its heart and find a happy compromise.

The hours unconsumed by work or play would be spent around a small coal fire in the living room listening to the radio or watching television. Occasionally my brother would be allowed to invite his friends over to watch 'the box', a treat that was gratefully accepted as television was relatively new to such rural areas. They would arrive in their Sunday best, hair Brylcreemed beyond belief, to sit in awe as 'Wagon Train' rumbled across the screen. Later they exited into the night touching forelocks and mumbling their thanks, a routine drilled home by parents intent that their offspring should make a good impression on anyone fortunate enough to own a television.

Major household utilities were sorely lacking on the farm and the luxury of a bathtub was something we had left behind. In its place was a tin tub dragged out once a week and set up in front of the fire. Like any small boy I abhorred being scrubbed down and continually had to be coaxed into the water with a guarantee that I would be allowed to listen to 'Biggles' and 'Flash Gordon' before being sent to bed. We had the same problem with the toilet, for when we arrived there was none and it was up to Dad to provide one for us. While we were spared the privy in the garden, what we got instead was a privy in the cellar. It was a sight to behold! Emerald green and made of tin, it sat like an electric chair at the bottom of the stairs, daring you to be seated. Behind it, yards of corrugated piping snaked up and disappeared out a small window high above: its purpose ventilation, its overall appearance that of a psychedelic steam engine.

Almost as unpleasant was the chore of collecting eggs, something I avoided whenever possible. Confronting these clucking birds with their irritating toilet habits and ferocious beaks became increasingly unappealing and gradually I came to develop an intense dislike for them. If ever it was possible for me to play hookey from my chores, you could usually find me exploring the local region astride my invisible steed.

All around me large open fields rose and fell beneath the hard

12

northern sky. Corn and barley flew their yellow flags and muddy cow-paths cut through thick copses housing partridge and pheasant. Rabbits and hares scythed through the vegetation like precision machinery devouring everything in their path. Come November, it was not uncommon to hear the endless barrage of gunfire as these creatures were thinned by armies of irritated farmers.

Following a narrow path downhill, I clambered over a stile leading into a muddy field sitting in the left-hand corner of our property and manoeuvred forward with trepidation until I reached a kissing-gate 200 yards ahead. The reason for my cautious behaviour was a nasty-looking sow of about 300 pounds reclining in the mud. I imagined this ordeal as Theseus facing the Minotaur, but in reality it was small Bernie facing large pig. As predator moved in on transgressor, I wondered why, when there was a perfectly safe alternative route to my destination, I chose to endure humiliation at the hoofs of this rotund porker. It could only be a child's fantasy to flirt with danger, although I never stayed around long enough to turn and slay my mythical beast, my feet constantly winning any battle with my brain.

This obstacle crossed and once more on neutral ground, I fell exhausted on to a flat rectangular field called the Todmoor which served year round as the local sportsground. Here, surrounded by a trickling stream, village pitted itself against village in feats of athletic prowess. In winter, red-faced young men bore down on each other, cursing and yelling for possession of a solitary leather ball, while in summer the same youths garbed in their whites curbed their tempers in the genteel art of willow on leather. At the weekends, locals gathered on the sidelines. Huddled in groups with their cloth caps pulled down over their eyes and their Parkies tight between their teeth, they encouraged their sides with grunts of approval and disappointment. My father had a habit of chastizing the players in a loud voice that embarrassed me and, hearing some of the choice comments hurled back, I felt it safer to watch from a distance.

For now, though, the only sound invading the silence was the distant lowing of a solitary Friesian. Picking myself up, I continued my trek across the Todmoor and over the small stone bridge separating it from the next field. On this bridge, at one time or another, I had assumed the role of Horatius defending

13

Rome from the Tuscan horde. The small stream had become the foaming Tiber while John Spaulding had become Astur, the great Lord of Luna, 'upon whose ample shoulders clanged the four-fold shield'.

You may have perceived that my games were far from mundane, as for me the simplicity of cops and robbers or cowboys and Indians lacked spice and originality. They involved one-dimensional characters born out of comic books and television. Not that I objected to these media, for they furnished me with basic heroes. But I preferred to embellish and improve their plots, taking them a step farther than the hail of imaginary bullets between points A and B. My preference was for the swashbucklers of poetry and prose. Always having been an incurable romantic, I felt that the bravado of Lochinvar and the daring of the Light Brigade painted a far more colourful picture than the slick soulless characters of detective drama.

The ground took an uphill swing and I found myself bracing against the incline until it levelled out into a mole-infested field circled by a high hedgerow riddled with rabbit holes. From here I viewed Bramby and the surrounding countryside in one panoramic sweep. It lay naked to the elements, its tiny church turret sprouting from the cottages like a seal of authenticity. This was, without a doubt, a place I loved to visit. Wild and windswept, it was a good place to gather your thoughts or mull over the problems of the day. Not many ventured here – only those unfortunates who had missed the last bus to Bixby could be seen using this alternative route home. For hours I would sit among the remains of the Angel Tree, the last surviving limbs of a local legend. It was said that long ago an angel of the Lord had descended and taken up residence in this tree. Confronting a local shepherd seeking refuge beneath its boughs, the angel had passed on to him a vital message from God to mankind. The shepherd returned to the village with this message, only to be stoned and exiled as a blasphemous madman. He later died in poverty taking with him the words of the divine messenger. I dreamed here and drew the evening air into my lungs. It was good to be young, experiencing nature at first hand. I lusted for life and lived each day to the full, all child in a world slowly slipping from a child's hands.

Like a dead leaf out of our lives,
we will leave this place with its secret walls
and its tell-tale heart deep inside.

Standing on a quiet village corner anywhere in Lincolnshire early on an autumn morning with the dew still heavy on the leaves, you're sure to see rag-tag groups of beefy housewives wrapped in greatcoats and headscarves. Coughing and wheezing, they greet each other with raucous remarks as they board ramshackle vans and lorries, which splutter off leaving clouds of blue fumes to evaporate in the cold morning air. What might look like a gang of peasants off to the labour camps is in fact a crew of potato-pickers going to work, and a hardier bunch of souls you are unlikely to meet. I'll never understand why I signed on for this barbaric form of slavery, and if there was any manual labour designed to break the spirit as well as the back, this was it. For a ten-year-old in need of extra pocket money it was sheer torture – the fingers blistered, the nails cracked, the body ached from head to toe. Great clods of thick soil stuck to my boots, restricting my manoeuvres and cramping my legs. The stints appeared to grow wider and the tractor seemed to return with increasing regularity as the day wore on. The handles on the wire baskets cut into my palms and pulled me down as the wind and sleet lashed at my face. The pace was frantic and any attempt to rest only incurred the wrath of our far from feminine gang-boss. This was my first paying job, if the mere pittance paid could be called a wage. Looking back, it is almost criminal to think how little one received for the hours worked. A day's sweat then wouldn't pay for a pint in today's inflated times. I'll admit I stuck with it and it did put some muscle in my arm and some determination in my heart, but eventually I handed in my tatty carrier and returned 'beyond the fields we know'.

Every Sunday morning we piled into the car and drove into Market Slaten to attend Mass. Without sounding irreverent, I don't believe any small child likes being turfed out of a warm bed and driven seven miles to sit rigid on a bench listening to a listless sermon in a draughty church. I've yet to meet anyone who felt the pulse of Christianity coursing through their veins at such a young age. Still, Sundays weren't all that bad, and we made our way home along the winding country lanes contemplating the awaiting aroma of roast beef and Yorkshire pudding. After lunch we would switch on the wireless and settle down to an afternoon's entertainment, beginning with Billy Cotton bellowing 'Wakey, wakey'. Through the long lazy hours we pottered with our hobbies as Dad dozed off and on beside the fire. The familiar voices of Kenneth Horne, Bill Pertwee and Jimmy Clitheroe entered the room and made us smile, till the Sunday paper slipped from my father's hands and we quietly tucked away our toys and climbed the stairs to bed.

When Father informed the family that he intended to build a new home on our property, we were ecstatic. His decision to attempt this Herculean task impressed me tremendously. In my eyes he had always been a man capable of fixing anything, but building a home was something I assumed you left to professionals. Once more I was proved incorrect and in a five-month period at the staggeringly low cost of £1,000 he erected an adorable, three-bedroom bungalow. The pioneer spirit had motivated our souls and on a crisp New Year's Day in 1960 we stepped over the threshold of a new home and into a new decade.

Two

Golden sand receded into deep gullies where weathered commandos lay in wait for the Desert Fox. Lifeless brittle trees crumbled under the tracks of Sherman tanks carving a path for Patton across the parched desert. All the glory, all those medals won and worn by gnarled GIs waging war on an eight-by-four tabletop in a dying house! By now I was deeply rooted in the toy soldier phase and comfortably ensconced in a new home. The swift flit had left our previous dwelling empty and it stood desperately trying to fight off dismantlement at the hands of time.

Seeing definite potential in the empty building, I moved in with my troops. Dad must have had the same idea, for as I entered armed with boxes of infantry, I was confronted by bags of chicken feed stacked along the walls from floor to ceiling. Settling for one of the smaller back rooms, I placed a large steel tabletop on two wooden horses. This was the foundation on which I would design and direct my war games. I was industrious in my construction and managed to incorporate no end of natural resources. I dampened down soil for a Somme-like effect and piled rocks strategically into replicas of alpine valleys, while twigs and branches became fallen trees enhancing the landscape. If my thieving fingers managed to filch a bag of flour, I could easily stage a snowy defeat for the Germans at Monte Cassino. I derived great pleasure from my little plastic figures and would spend hours hovering above them like some heavenly general. My hands reached into the home-made terrain and advanced or retreated my men as the mood took me. The decision was mine, whether they should charge to victory or be flicked to the ground by the finger of fate.

My desire for realism was questionable and my parents drew the line when I took to dousing my soldiers with lighter-fluid in order to simulate flamethrower attacks. Another practice that was none too intelligent was pouring gunpowder out of penny bangers into the barrels of my howitzers. Once ignited, this had an impressive effect. However, I noticed that along with an alarming loss of eyebrows, the gunpowder was slowly melting my cannons until they were little more than twisted chunks of green lead. My indulgence in these manoeuvres entertained me and taught me the art of strategy, until the day I fell prey to a marble shark who demanded the bulk of my troops in payment for his victory. One by one the rest vanished, either lost or misplaced; like true soldiers they faded heroically along with my interest. Later my battlefield was dismantled and the room cleared. As for my fascination with what we now termed the Old House, it had barely been tapped and was to see many more of my projects before its date with the wrecking ball.

A strange obsession filled the stone
that ached in pleasure 'round this building.

By now I was in my final year of primary school which I attended in the neighbouring village of Doramby-by-Huddle. All that kept the two villages apart was a short stretch of about 500 yards lined on one side by cherry trees planted in 1953 to commemorate the Coronation. In early summer they were laden with beautiful blossom that filled my nostrils with its bouquet as I walked to school each morning. The school was an uninteresting building of somewhat indecisive architecture. There were two classrooms, one for little 'uns and one for big 'uns. The former were instructed by a lanky pinched-faced woman called Miss Picson who favoured recorder recitals and punished her pupils by pulling them up from their seats by their sideburns. The big 'uns were taught by the headmaster, Mr Holborne, an imposing man with right-wing leanings and a streak of sarcasm. He would lecture us periodically on the evils of pop and the alarming rise of what he termed ' . . . this jungle music'. He also had a bizarre resentment of chewing gum, which he continually referred to as 'black men's toenails' after witnessing native workers trampling chicle in some obscure BBC documentary. I think he wished to believe he was an enlightened man steering us along the path of virtue, but in fact his sermons tended to be statements born of conservative one-sidedness. This might have done irreparable damage had we been attentive students but, following the norm, everything went in one ear and out the other, saving us from his outdated Victorian morality. Mr Holborne's main effort was to cram as much knowledge as possible into the limited space between our ears in order to prime us for the impending eleven-plus which would decide where our continued education took us.

The prospect of moving on had not yet sunk in, as I was more interested in the arrival of my new brother who appeared, pink and screaming, into a midwife's hands early in the spring of 1961. The build-up to this had been fairly uneventful and curiosity had set in only when the hustle and bustle around the house had unhinged my routine. No matter where I placed myself I was constantly in the way, and it was with a chip of indignation on my shoulder that I retreated into the Old House to engage the enemy at Iwo Jima. I spent much of my time here while the action at home came to boiling point. Soon the stork arrived and I immediately took on the role of proud and doting brother, and with cryptic descriptions informed one and all of the wondrous event. Like everything else, the novelty soon wore off and I went about my business ignoring his constant bawling and nasty toilet habits.

One of my acquaintances at this point was an oily unattractive boy called Martin Swilley who was some years older than I. Martin was a loner and unpopular with most people in the village. I sensed that even my parents, who were very liberal, found him rather offensive. I was not sure what it was about him that repelled people, and it was this curiosity that sent me apple-scrumping with him. Our target was the orchard of an irritable old fossil whose garden lay at the bottom of Pump Hill on the outskirts of Bramby. As dusk descended we scrambled through the space in his hedge to gorge ourselves on his best Granny Smiths. We sat hidden among the trees as Martin expounded on a number of subjects, leaving me with the distinct impression that he was not as tightly wrapped as I had at first imagined. Excitedly, his eyes glistened through a greasy cowlick as he told me endless stories of ritualistic mayhem in faraway countries; tales of weird cults and barbaric ceremonies performed by godless creatures on distant continents. Sweat trickled down his fleshy nose and dangled precariously at its tip, as in vivid detail he described the carnal practices of Zulus and Pygmies. His knowledge of such atrocities was frightening, but worse was his total enjoyment of them as he revelled in graphic description like some verbal 'Mondo Carne'. Martin knew the ins and outs of all things unpleasant and it was through this sordid informant that I discovered how my new brother had been conceived. His explicit half-truths on sex seemed hard to swallow and, if indeed these were the facts of life, then you could leave them to the birds and bees.

One day I asked Martin where he gained this wealth of bizarre information and was shocked to learn it was through his friend Jocko. Jocko was the local hermit who lived in an abandoned mill house on a desolate piece of land between the two villages. An enigma, like many eccentrics, Jocko was regarded as both madman and vagrant. It really shouldn't have surprised me then that if Jocko was Martin's mentor, he was definitely worth steering clear of. True to form, however, when Martin offered to take me to visit the recluse, I accepted. It was an episode that was to end my friendship with Martin Swilley, proving that he truly was the juvenile Uriah Heep everyone imagined him to be.

To get to Jocko's house we had to follow a two-mile path running parallel to the main road joining Bramby and Doramby. Although a little apprehensive, I had put on a brave face for Martin's benefit. It was a beautiful day and I was intoxicated by the aromatic scents of nature surrounding me. The air was full of birdsong, as tits and finches hopped among the gooseberry bushes pecking at the tart fruit. Midges flitted in mad circles above muddy puddles pitted unevenly along the trail. The hedgerows and ditches bordering the path were wild and overgrown and deserted allotments lay dying, choked by the irrepressible onslaught of rye grass and cocksfoot. Greenhouses vandalized by veteran village yobos stood like metal skeletons allowing tendrils of clinging ivy to crawl around their rusted frames – like Sleeping Beauty residing in slumber, forgotten by time.

We reached Jocko's by midday and were ignored by two emaciated guard dogs engaged in a snarling stand-off over the remains of some small animal. Jocko's old van standing in the

20

driveway informed us that he was home, and without hesitating Martin marched up to the door and knocked. Instantly the door opened and there was Jocko grinning apishly through a set of decaying yellow teeth. Although his appearance was insanitary, his manner seemed friendly enough. Politely I refused his offer of sardine sandwiches and condensed milk, a combination that could only have appealed to an Andes plane-crash survivor. As Martin and Jocko conversed on nothing in particular, I took in my surroundings. The interior of the cottage reflected its owner, untidy and dirty, the bare essentials of survival scattered throughout.

Jocko eked out a living breeding rabbits, and from where I stood I could see his hutches lined up one on top of the other. Whether he bred them for fun or for fur, I never discovered, for it was at this point that the two of them started snickering heavily. I managed to overhear snatches of 'Agh, go on, show him.'

'I dunno, he's a young 'un.'

'He's all right, he won't snitch.'

My interest aroused, I inquired what it was they were talking about. At my insistence they looked at each other with a distinct 'Shall we?', obviously deciding that it was okay. Jocko nodded with a knowing smile and left the room. I asked Martin what he'd gone to fetch and received only a mute smirk in return. The panic button at the back of my head was registering a warning and I began to get a little worried. Just as I was about to make some excuse to leave, Jocko returned clutching a grubby oilskin pouch. He fumbled at the knot around the package with what little was left of his cracked and filthy fingernails. I sat rigid, prepared for the worst and unable to imagine how the contents of this tatty pouch could be worth the visit. Jocko removed what looked like a stack of grainy photographs much the worse for the passing of time. I could see the corners were clearly worn from constant handling as he handed me the top picture and said, 'Ever seen anythin' like 'at?' I stared at the photo unable to comprehend what it was I was seeing amongst the entwined naked bodies. Slowly my eyes studied it from top to bottom as a prickly feeling began to crawl up my spine and uncontrollably my lip began to quiver.

One by one the dirty pictures were pushed on to my lap and a world of grotesque pornography was opened up. Copulating couples in all forms of human degradation lay before me in black and white. Swarthy Latins with abnormally large organs cradled in their palms paraded their gender in front of salacious Fatimas reclining in oceans of cellulite. All this ugliness flashed before me as Martin sniggered asides about the uncommon size of the male genitalia. I had never seen anything like this and what upset me most was the seedy secrecy in which it all transpired. Everything about it was cheap and dirty, not just the pictures but Martin, Jocko, the house and the nauseating smell of sardines. It was all so unclean. How could these people exhibit their bodies in this fashion? Weren't they embarrassed? Had they no shame? All these impressions flashed through my mind as I clutched their smut in my trembling fingers. Willing these images to dissipate, I managed to ignore their filth and blind myself with the thin film of tears that covered my eyes. As the flow of Jocko's smut came to an end, I made the decision that I would not reward them with a reaction of shock. Taking a deep breath, I stood up stiffly, muttered something like 'not bad' and left. Once outside I expelled a sigh of relief and ran as if the devil himself were on my tail. Home was the only place I wished to be right now; pornography could wait.

The garden surrounding our new bungalow was blossoming and my mother's green fingers added hints of colour at every turn. After the arduous task of pregnancy came a renewed interest in the garden. In the afternoons as she weeded and pruned, the burden of babysitting was borne by several village girls. Billing and cooing over our bundle of joy, they trundled off with his pram, happy as mother hens. Presumably he acted as a more realistic plaything than their own plastic facsimiles. I often wondered what they did with him in the hours they were gone, and I envisioned him being made to perform in all manner of sissy games before being returned home with a silly grin on his face.

Father's smallholding was also growing. In addition to the battery, he had now erected two broiler houses and several open-range runs. It seemed that the challenge had paid off and he worked from dawn to dusk with the ever-present shadow of Jill at his side. Faithful and obedient, Jill was man's best friend, anticipating my father's every command with soulful eyes. She had been given to me as a pup by a local shepherd and I had trailed her home on a yard of binder band. I pleaded with my parents to let me keep her and they relented on the condition that I maintain her welfare. This was fine for a while but, as usual, the responsibility soon fell back on them. I adored Jill, but with school taking up most of my time she soon turned to my father for companionship. This bond grew stronger with the years until she was an extension of my father himself.

Later, when my father sold the farm and became a civil servant, she would wait by the garage in all weathers until he returned home each evening. Even when age turned off her sight and closed her ears to sound, she still sensed his presence and remained his shadow. We were shattered when she died, none more so than my father. In true tradition, he showed little exterior emotion but deep inside he was crushed. Jill was a part of my growing up for more than sixteen years and her death was like the loss of a dear friend.

> . . . four feet of ground in front of the barn
> that's sun-baked and rain-soaked and part of the farm.

From time to time I was prodded by the spirit of adventure and one challenge was to climb the tower of the local church, a medieval structure seemingly untouched since the last Saxon char-lady cleaned up in the twelfth century. Although the outer structure was sound, the inner ladders and floors leading to the summit were as perilous as the well in a Lassie movie. Normally I attempted this climb as dusk touched the horizon and a clear cumulus sky retreated beyond the red sunset west of Lincoln. Like a Babylonian fire, it sprang from the countryside in a burst of amber and scarlet flame. I followed the short path down the centre of the graveyard, through the tall ragwort covering the long-deceased, to reach the entrance to the church. Once inside, all sound stopped. The stillness was overwhelming and the musty smell of ageing masonry filled my nostrils. To the left beyond the bell-ropes were the steps to the second level and, placing my feet lightly on the first rung, I began my ascent. Creaking timber broke the silence and gave advance warning to the rats above that an alien presence was invading their domain. Squeezing through the first trapdoor I was met by the oppressive heat of the tiny chamber constituting the second storey. A sense of claustrophobia drove me immediately upwards as I fumbled my way through the half-darkness towards the next ladder which led to the belfry. Here short blasts of cold air formed a chilling crossfire through the double lancet windows.

Large oak beams hewn by tools of little precision formed a brace for the two great bells bound by their obligation to toll for Christianity. Through a maze of timbers on the far side of the bells were the last remaining steps to the tower. On one occasion as I made my way across this network of beams I tripped and lurched forward, instinctively grabbing for the closest form of support. In that unfortunate instance it happened to be the bell-rope and, like Quasimodo, I swung to and fro as a resounding clang echoed through the village.

Once through the circular opening to the tower, I remained below the level of the balustrade to avoid detection by the curate. Small boys treading on hallowed ground could easily be mistaken for lead thieves. Cautiously I peered over the edge. The darkness limited my view and anything beyond the proximity of the Pig Market was little more than an ebony wash. The tiny cottages below me chugged pillowy clouds of smoke that bounced along the rooftops and melted into the air. Light flickered through the living-room curtains as nightfall heralded teatime and the end of the working day. An urgency bristled beneath me as the sound of good-natured camaraderie rang from door to door along the street. Something about this spirited cheerfulness made me warm with compassion and ravenous of stomach, requirements that could be dealt with only by the lights that keep the home fires burning. With a stub of candle to light my descent, I climbed back down from whence I came and headed home with a sense of accomplishment.

Where I lived there were no theatrical matinées and Saturday morning picture shows. We made the best of what time and the elements had given us – natural entertainment in nature's playground. I was hard-pressed to feel reluctant at missing the pleasures of cosmopolitan life. Cockcrow substituted for the scream of the factory whistle. Instead of the ashen hordes teeming from the mills and mines, I saw healthy colour and gentleness in the faces of simple tradesmen whose happy smiles greeted me each day. Ben the electrician would wave from his little green van, and George the scrapman would toss me a toffee as he clattered by with his horse and cart. There were dozens of them, the kind of people who can't live within the confines of routine regimentation. There were those who were mean, those who were comical and those who were downright eccentric. Mrs Ernestine Corbett would most definitely fit neatly into this last category. She was the spearhead of the Women's Institute, Red Cross troubleshooter and grand matriarch to we lesser mortals who dwelled around her ivory tower. The tower in this instance being the village's most impressive residence which she shared with her husband, Bertram. The home had once been occupied by the Lord of the Manor and was situated at the top of the village surrounded by several acres of rose gardens and rockeries.

The Corbetts were a formidable couple and, to the best of my recollection, were both extremely large. Bertram Corbett was robust and rotund, with an immense face and hands that made him resemble a gargantuan sponge puppet. Mrs Corbett, on the other hand, was of Nordic dimensions, statuesque and slightly bowed like the proud figurehead of some Viking longboat. He was a respected cattle-dealer in the community, while she was an unstoppable organizer of jumble sales, village fêtes and coffee-mornings. Her energy was boundless as she careered about the area behind the wheel of a large green Austin. Her driving skills were appalling and she would lay her hand upon the horn, continually forewarning pedestrians of her approach. She entered our lives from the moment we arrived in the village. No sooner had the moving van pulled out than she pulled in, intent on roping my mother into voluntary service. My mother had never been the WI charity biscuit-passing type, so her initial reaction was not entirely positive. However, she found the eccentric side of Mrs Corbett fascinating, having always been drawn to those a little left of centre. My father regarded her as an overbearing loony and retreated into hiding whenever she appeared. As time went by, a bizarre friendship blossomed between my mother and Mrs C., as she became known to us. There was a compassion in my mother that was drawn to this crusty but basically kind old dowager; while Mrs C. was attracted to my mother's fierce and intelligent non-conformity. Nurtured by these differences they would spend much time together, Mrs C. roaring down the road for morning coffee and my mother walking up to the big house for afternoon tea.

I was terrified of her – she seemed so awesome, with a way of making a request sound like an order. She was bossy, belligerent and determined that things be done her way or no way at all. But for all these negative traits, there was something that attracted me like a magnet to that big house. There, weeding and cleaning in her service, I would spend hours lost among the flower beds, raking the soil for little reward save the pleasure of spending time in this secret garden. It became a foreign country, a kingdom ruled by my hand. The house became my castle full of dusty attics and a multitude of rooms where no one dwelled. I set out on expeditions up back stairs to these forgotten places where I unearthed trunks filled with treasures. It might have been a pile of walking sticks, a faded photo album or a faceless doll, but to me it was Aladdin's cave and every article was a priceless discovery. I may have been nervous in the presence of Mrs C., but there was no doubt her heart was in the right place, for she never denied me access to her home with the exception of the days she entertained. In these instances she would shoo me off into the garden or the surrounding farmyard, where I would tag along behind Mr C. whom I adored. I could always count on him for plenty of attention, an abundance of sweets and rides on his enormous knees. He had a passion for those funny little games in glass cases where you had to get a series of silver balls into various holes. I would sit for what seemed like hours perched on his lap trying unsuccessfully to manoeuvre them, as he smiled at my progress while extracting a constant stream of Quality Street from his cavernous pockets.

My kingdom was a happy one but I soon yearned for the one thing it lacked – a queen. In answer to my prayers she arrived soon afterwards and the kingdom was complete. She was Mrs C.'s granddaughter Mary who lived in Nottingham with her sister Penny. The two of them came to visit one summer weekend and the palace was never the same again. That weekend, like Pip summoned by Miss Havisham in *Great Expectations*, I was ordered to come and play. Mary, like the porcelain beauty Estella, was stand-offish and slightly frosty, but soon warmed to me once she discovered my knack for make-believe, and readily complied to being moulded into all manner of heroines for my romantic leads.

Her sister Penny, like most younger siblings, was an appendage we did our best to discard. This was easier said than done and it was often necessary to cast her in minor roles. Mary and I became very close and in time made the standard childhood promises of faithfulness, cementing our pacts with elaborate rituals. We swore that when the years allowed, we would become husband and wife, a feeling that seemed so natural at the time. In pretence we married and via an immaculate conception gave birth to and raised Penny as our child. In this way we existed in a world of our own construction, happiness reigning sublime through the hot summer days. Alas though, as in all fairy tales, into our magic kingdom came a malcontent in the guise of John David, Mary's cousin. To begin with this invasion was not too traumatic as John David was even younger than Penny. However, he became more demanding as time went by, and before long it seemed that half of our time was spent calming him down when he discovered us and made a scene. Like some miniature usurper, he laid waste to our kingdom, causing us to become exiles in our own land. He had found the silver lining to our cloud and sewn it closed with sticky fingers.

Soon after this Mary went away to boarding school and her visits became few and far between. Things were never the same again and, unable to argue with time, we were forced to let it pull us apart. Our summer house promises whispered with conviction spiralled into the air and were lost among the rafters, where for all I know they still remain today.

My isolation from the real world was about to be axed neatly at the neck, sending the ball above my shoulders bouncing down the road to secondary school. I approached my eleven-plus with great trepidation, and sat in silence throughout the examination staring in alarm at the rambling problems posed by the pages of foolscap. Up to now I had managed deftly to fend off education as a necessary evil. I enjoyed certain aspects, such as composition and history, but my mind drew a blank the moment arithmetic reared its ugly head. It proved to be my downfall, and as I sat squinting at the symbols pertaining to addition and subtraction, the furrows in my brow grew deep and long. Endless diagrams and problems beginning 'If Bob had six oranges and Sue had two ...' remained unsolved as I filled the answer boxes with unintelligible doodles. Of course, I failed miserably.

My parents were informed that come September their second son would not be attending grammar school, but would be taking the low road to life's rich opportunities via Market Slaten Secondary Modern, the legendary underbelly of education. They bore the news honourably and I'm sure were less than impressed at my achievement, but they resigned themselves to the fact that one out of two wasn't bad. My older brother had passed his eleven-plus with flying colours the previous year and was now a bona-fide smarty at Temple Lord Grammar School. My heart went out to him, for while his classmates' younger brothers were following in their footsteps, his dumbo brother had to go and get 'a one-way ticket to Palookaville'. So with my fate in the hands of the inevitable first term, I decided to make the summer holiday prior to my indoctrination a memorable one. Perhaps it was unintentional, but I have a feeling that since I had discovered failure so admirably, there was no reason on earth why I shouldn't take it one step farther. I discovered rock and roll.

The first time I became aware of records was in 1957 when we journeyed to London to visit my uncle and aunt in Putney. This was my father's side of the family and they had many sons ranging in age and height, whose roster of names read like a roll-call of French saints. My boisterous friendly cousins with their big smiles and European charm treated 'little green in the big city' with courtesy and kindness; but with a language barrier inbuilt between us, I was out in the cold when it came to conversation. Having little else to occupy my time, I discovered their record player and a stock of old seventy-eights. Through this archaic sound system I first heard the lines 'I got pig iron, I got pig iron, I got all pig iron', as Lonnie Donegan told the story of 'The Rock Island Line'. I was hooked, and every day I sat religiously before the turntable clinging to the narrative of the skiffle man's song. I would play and replay 'John Henry', 'The Grand Coolie Dam' and 'Have a Drink on Me' until they were word perfect in my mind. In this quiet London suburb, I had become a fan and discovered my first singing idol.

Tune me in to the wild side of life . . .

As the summer of '61 unfurled a floral banner over the warm Lincolnshire countryside, a new animal was breaking through the bars of a bland cage called the American Forces Network. Among the homogenized pop I taped on our cumbersome reel-to-reel were urgent examples of teenage repression. Pat Boone's 'Johnny Will' and Paul Anka's 'Puppy Love' were eclipsed by tough kids singing, *'If the folks come home, I'm afraid they're gonna have my hide ...'* and how *' ... there'd be no more movies for a week or two, no more running 'round with the usual crew'* but *' ... who cares, C'mon Everybody'.* I had been listening to and taping regularly the candy-coated recordings of Bobby Vee and Bryan Hyland, while somewhere on that dial could be found the likes of Eddie Cochran and Little Richard. Out here in the country trends took their time in arriving, and with the censors concerning themselves with the protection of our morals and the welfare of our being, it was tough to find good rock and roll along the wavelengths.

As the months followed one another, justice prevailed and the milk-toasts were forced to retreat before the onslaught of leather jackets and greasy kids stuff. Even mainstream pop had taken a turn for the better with singers of the calibre of Sam Cooke. Those such as Del Shannon and the Everly Brothers maintained a high standard, while the awesome voice of Roy Orbison was impossible to ignore, delivering a hauntingly passionate 'Running Scared'. At the same time I still retained my love of narrative ballads. Johnny Horton's 'North to Alaska' and Johnny Cash's 'Ring of Fire' made their mark, but it was when I heard Marty Robbins's bitter-sweet tale of 'El Paso' that I knew there was a happy medium between rock and the written word. This picturesque song meshed perfectly with my sense of adventure and I yearned for the badlands of New Mexico. And while Hayley Mills had everyone singing 'Let's Get Together', *'Night-time would find me in Rosa's Cantina'.*

As music surged and settled itself before a craving audience, I was looking to my future with dubious concern. I had discovered a new light that had burst forth like a rising inner flame. Youth had a real chance to communicate through music, but in music – like all games of chance – a price had to be paid. In April 1960 Eddie Cochran died when his limousine collided with a lamp-post south of London, and a year earlier a plane carrying the innovative Buddy Holly had crashed in a field near Fargo, North Dakota. Rock had been born in my soul, the Sixties were taking shape, and the body count had begun.

Three

My parents' decision to buy me the optional uniform of my new school was a nice thought, but as I boarded the bus the morning of my first term I felt as if a sign reading 'unclean' had been hung around my neck. Those before me shrunk away at the sight of the gold crest emblazoned upon my breast-pocket, as I searched in vain among my fellow-travellers for some replica of my own attire. All around me swirled a wild array of leather and denim and I quickly took a seat, attempting to become invisible, aware that new boys were looked upon with disdain. Hot breath and callous eyes swept across me and I wished that I could strangle my parents in payment for their generosity.

It was seven miles to Market Slaten and a twisting lane took us through several hamlets and passed many lonely farmhouses before reaching the main road. The traffic was heavier here as other buses converged on to the highway with their howling cargo hanging out the windows. Market Slaten was a pleasant place known primarily for its racecourse, and it had a certain charm that made it stand out among the towns that lined the main road to the coast. A population of about 9,000 worked in and about this industrious warren of Georgian and Victorian houses, and a cavalcade of friendly shop-fronts beckoned a brisk family business on market days and weekends.

The area was diverse in its appeal, and while it was easy to find silver birch and conifers standing in thick purple heather to the north, the greyer south side had the secondary modern trapped neatly between the gas works and the plastics factory. It was in this depressing area that we disembarked and, like resolute lambs to the slaughter, joined the heaving snake filtering through the front gates. One by one my travelling companions shunted off into familiar packs leaving me alone and out of my depth. I was naked in a new world, unprotected by the wings that enveloped me in times of crisis. My imaginary weapons melted in the heat of reality and the vivid realms of the classics seemed dwarfed by the crude instructive formats that faced me now. I thrust my hands into my pockets and pushed my way into the crowd as the unceremonious clang of the school bell beckoned us to assembly.

The school was a sprawling maze of buildings, each of a different period and design. The original block was fronted by a wide veranda that surrounded a garden bordered by flower beds. At one end, a stone stairway led to the main hall and through to the rear quadrangle, and off to the left running parallel to the playing field were several converted Nissen huts. Adjacent to the front gates next to the canteen, a new library and several classrooms had been built the previous year. Like Nazis screening their atrocities from the Red Cross, the Board of Governors had hidden antiquation behind a veneer of progress. In fact, with a little barbed wire and a couple of gun turrets, our school could have doubled nicely for Dachau or Treblinka.

The trauma of adjusting to my new surroundings was not the ordeal I had expected and within a few days I managed to blend in unobtrusively. I even befriended several of my classmates when we realized that, being in the same boat, there was validity to the theory of safety in numbers. The first few weeks were spent familiarizing ourselves with our timetable and dodging the constant bullying of the older boys. There was a tradition of 'ducking', which involved the christening of newcomers by sticking their head in a toilet bowl and pulling the chain. This was a ritual I went to great lengths to escape, and for the first month my friends and I could be found hiding out in the far corners of the playing field, or huddled together in the darkest recesses of the changing room. From here we heard the pitiful screams of the captured, and caught glimpses of their flailing limbs as they were dragged to their annointment by their would-be baptists. This was the only period in my five years at school when I actually looked forward to class, for once under instruction I attained a temporary amnesty from the brutal custom of initiation.

. . . sitting in the classroom trying to look intelligent . . .

The teaching staff either teetered on the verge of eccentricity or fell fully into the category of lunacy. There were those who believed their profession was a calling to be taken seriously, and those who seriously believed that their calling was the only way to make a living. Some felt violence was an alternative to their lack of skill, while others merely tolerated disobedience and went through the motions as insanity raged around them. One had to sympathize, as the majority of their students would sooner eat their pencils than write with them, and the overall consensus of the teaching body was that this place was merely a holding tank for apprentice philistines. There was little belief that anything more than tractor drivers and factory hands inhabited their classrooms, and any effort to increase what little knowledge lay in our almost dormant brains was better left at home.

Seeing the pupil through a teacher's eyes could indeed be frightening. The boys branched pretty much into two categories, the thick and the thicker. Here, intelligence was not a require-ment for survival, and while certain elements were the smooth athletic type with their knitted ties and Denson points, it was the physically gargantuan most of us feared. Varying in age, they were abnormal in size and could be recognized by their penchant for horrendous hobnailed boots, which caused sparks to fly from the granite walkway whenever they approached. Heavy denims with twelve-inch turn-ups were held at the waist by thick leather belts with ugly-looking buckles, perfect for persuading the meek to disinherit their dinner money. It was best to remain on the good side of these types and many did so by becoming minions to their every command. During breaks these greasy turncoats could be seen scuttling about on errands, while their masters stood around in hulking groups chain-smoking Woodbines and revving great spitballs into the backs of passing students. Any teacher imagining a smack across the head could solve a problem did so at his own peril if the object of that blow was one of these bullies. If the target was feeling grumpy that day, the teacher might find himself embedded in the blackboard.

While the boys asserted their masculinity, the girls spent inordinate amounts of time behind their compacts, tarting themselves up and admiring their blossoming figures. In a haze of perfumed mist, these lacquered doxies backcombed their hair into teetering beehives while expounding on the misfortunes of young love. Chewing vast quantities of Chiclets, their skinny fingers flicked through the pages of *Mirabelle*, delivering critiques on the latest adventures of Doctor Kildare. Squealing at the mention of Elvis and other current idols, their satchels and school books bore the names of their heroes stencilled in ink and surrounded by hearts of red crayon. Broadening their outlook meant little to them and their presence here was merely a formality. They ached to trade in their gym shorts for a nylon smock and to take their place on the assembly line. I often wondered if there wasn't a chute under our school that led straight to the plastics factory. I imagined them lined up before the headmaster on the last day of term as he patted them on the head and pulled a lever at his side, sending them down a slide and on to the line. Their fate was to marry young and bear the offspring of husbands who ignored them and used them with diminishing frequency, until their tattered lives left them bitter and hurt, tending home in some council-house complex.

I must make it clear that I am dealing with the majority and generalizing to a certain degree. Among the hundreds who came and went there were those who aspired to greater things, but to gain a closer understanding of the British secondary system of the Sixties it is necessary to detail it in retrospect as seen through my eyes. I would be fooling myself to pretend that within our school there might have existed Pasteurs, Tennysons and Churchills. In my own way I was equally as uninspired, and it was only later in life that I realized that in order to escape this conformity it was a case of sink or swim.

The subjects taught by our reluctant teaching staff were bland fare: the standard reading, writing and my old enemy arithmetic. Foreign languages were completely ignored and in their place was a subject more apropos of the area. Under the misleading label of agricultural science we were taught gardening, a subject I felt was instigated to attain free labour to tend the grounds. For a subject of this nature you would expect the calm gentle instruction of the Percy Thrower type, as in a soft Shropshire burr he would tell us how 'Thart goes thar' and 'My, ain't them bagonias bootiful?' Here that would have been like offering an exposed arm to a mad dog. Instead, we got Mr Cash.

Mr Cash was not one of my favourite human beings. I abhorred any form of gardening and truly believed he disliked me intensely, regarding me as a wimp with aspirations above the sod and turf. Above all, he had a ferocious temper backed with a voice of astronomical power that could part a head of hair at a hundred yards. With his hands firmly clasped behind his back, he strode through the furrows in his houndstooth tweeds overseeing the hoeing and mowing like some strutting commandant. Favouritism was evident in the garden and it was not paranoia on my part that constantly had me weeding while the bully boys got to drive the motor plough and paint the toolshed. Mr Cash took no chances and endeared himself to the tougher element by forming them into an élite group of private pets.

Once I had the misfortune to meet Mr Cash's wrath full force in a physical rather than verbal sense. While racing to the tuck shop one day, a friend and I had unintentionally ploughed down his neighbour's young daughter. We apologized profusely to the child's mother, but feeling this was not enough she complained about our conduct to the headmaster. In assembly the next day our names were called out and before the entire school we were chastised for our inconsiderate behaviour. With our embarrassment complete we began our first class, which just happened to be gardening. Mr Cash, believing the punishment we had just received was inadequate, decided that retribution was in order. Dismissing the class, he detained my friend and I and commenced hurling us from one end of the room to the other. With veins protruding dangerously from the neck and forehead of his scarlet face, he pummelled us with his fists. Like limbless dolls we ricocheted off the walls lined with implements, sending rows and rows of the finest spades and hoes into orbit until our punishment had run its course. I never felt that our crime warranted such action. The whole episode shows how the power of education in the wrong hands can be misused, and a violent temper merely made up for the lack of a better solution.

Believe it or not, there were those who were actually less qualified to teach than Mr Cash. There was a small Irishman called O'Flaherty who arrived one day as a substitute teacher, only to depart a week later a gibbering dishevelled wreck. It was not hard to detect that he was, as they say, not short of a few bob. The cut of his suits was not the regulation sag and hang, and his transport was far above the Morris Minor standard. Before our eyes we watched as his cocky exterior began to disintegrate under

34

the din of disinterested rabble. After a few days of this his decorum collapsed, and within minutes the façade fell as he began to leap up and down like some demented leprechaun. In a fit of hysterics, he made the fatal mistake of laying the flat side of a ruler to the lobe of Bonehead, the school's number one animal. With a cold stare of disbelief, Bonehead slowly rose from his seat cradling his attacked ear. Towering above the tiny teacher, he calmly removed the ruler from O'Flaherty's hand and crumbled it like matchwood in his fingers. The next thing we knew, our helpless teacher was being transported by giant hands above our heads in the direction of the corner closet. Unceremoniously Bonehead flung the irate Irishman into the cupboard and locked the door. The rest of the morning was spent in idle conversation as his muffled screams for help were ignored.

There were several teachers whose lessons I enjoyed. One in particular, Mr Roach, taught us history. He was not only an imposing sight to behold but possessed an eccentric sense of the absurd. He seemed out of character for our school and would have been more at home within the hallowed walls of Eton or Rugby. With his waxed moustache and heavy tweeds he arrived each day in a vintage Bentley, aloof but never pompous, to instruct us in the history of the world. With slow sweeping gestures, his eyes rolling dramatically, he did his utmost to improve our knowledge of the past. I saw in him some inner passion for all things bygone, for while he took us laboriously through the stages of our evolution I sensed the tell-tale signs that he was lost in the past. Even though he appeared distant, he was always in control of his class, and one of his more bizarre habits was hurling a large throwing-knife into the desks of unattentive pupils. This he did with great dexterity and was able to pin an exercise book to a desk top without moving from his position at the front of the room. Needless to say, this habit commanded a certain amount of respect.

No man's a jester playing Shakespeare . . .

By the end of the first term I was entrenched in the system and looking forward to the Christmas holidays. I had made several friends during the first few months and one of them was close enough to call a pal. With the consent of my parents I was allowed to have him over for the weekend. His name was Peter Cale and he lived on the RAF base at Woolworth, three miles from Bramby. He was a tall well-groomed boy and one of the few who also owned the official school blazer. His father, being in the Air Force, expected him to behave in a manner befitting the son of a military man, while his mother expected a full run-down on my parents' character and class status before he was allowed to pack his toothbrush. We passed the inspection and that winter I brought home my first house-guest.

Lincolnshire winters could be heavy and bitter and in Bramby the snow settled quickly, sweeping into deep drifts that barred the way of traffic and prevented deliveries. Mangolds and sugar beet froze in the open ground as the earth turned solid, cutting off the life support of the plants and increasing the workload of the industrious animals of the field. The farmers, like the animals, fought the elements, protecting their stock and maintaining their machinery in the hollow fury of blizzard and wind. Even in the midst of this bleakness one could not help but admire the beauty, as large flakes of virgin snow tumbled from the December skies, forming layer upon layer of white tears in the cradle of the countryside. To us the snow meant only fun and while our elders complained, we complied with the rules laid out by our seasonal host. The snowmen grew and the snowballs flew as Peter and I ran the gauntlet of each other's tactics. Our farm contained many splendid hiding places, but the pureness of the snow illuminated our every shadow and there was little chance of going undetected. Our excited voices echoed against the still landscape until dusk descended and we retired to the comfort of hot baths and fresh sheets. When the weather outside refused to settle and the storms of sleet and hail pounded the tiles above us, we kept abreast of pop by watching 'Six-Five Special' and 'Oh Boy'.

The faces on the screen were familiar by now, but the copycatting of the American Top Fifty by English singers was endless. Cliff Richard remained top dog and was at least original in his material, but it was disappointing to see the more rebellious performers like Billy Fury reverting to cover versions of tame American hits. At this time, Elvis was at the tail end of greatness and songs such as 'Wooden Doll' and 'Rock a Hula Baby' lacked his original commitment. There was a void in rock that was not being filled, and for the time being we had little choice. Helen

Shapiro was 'Walking Back to Happiness' and Wink Martindale was laying out his 'Deck of Cards'. The occasional burst of Chuck Berry caused me to kick up my heels, but like many others I awaited a sign from some new Messiah.

Peter didn't share my passion for music and I had the feeling he thought me a little strange for being interested in something associated with girls mooning over manufactured sissies. I couldn't have cared less, and the following summer I badgered him into donning a leather jacket. My brother took pictures of us posing on an upturned chicken crate, striking pop star stances with a couple of battered guitars. Once Peter saw these photos he changed his tune, and I never saw him wear his blazer again. He began turning up for school in a variety of teddy boy attire which his father was less than pleased about and probably he blamed me for instigating this delinquency in his son. Although I'm sure I aided and abetted Peter, something leads me to believe that by this time he too had seen the light. After this incident he never came to stay again and, though we remained friends, we both sought out new acquaintances, or in my case accomplices.

One of winter's great attributes was that life became increasingly difficult for the school bus. It was expected each morning at eight and the rule was that if it had not arrived by eight-thirty it was acceptable to return home, presuming the bus had found the roadway impenetrable. We prayed for this situation and diligently made the trek to the bus stop each morning. Every second was counted down till the hand hit the half-hour, leaving little else but our breath hanging in the air. Not even the distant sound of the diesel engine or the horn blaring could keep us rooted to the spot once the time was up. There was many a morning our driver saw the disappearing bums of fleeing schoolboys as he brought the bus to a halt at eight-thirty-one. The thought of a day free of chilling classrooms and irritable teachers was far too pleasurable to be spoiled by commendable behaviour.

The reason I disliked manual subjects and active sports was that I seemed to be constantly handed the short end of the stick. Like my relegation to weeding in the agricultural department, so too I was alienated from the front line when it came to sports. I was certainly not the best soccer player or the finest batsman, but I did possess a wiry physique and natural agility, which if put to use might have been of some help. This particular assessment of my prowess went unappreciated by our gamesmaster, who found me a far more suitable candidate for target practice. As I shivered between two posts, the first eleven bombarded me with balls to improve their aim and, if necessary, vent their hostility. Little more than a tall dwarf at the time, this hardship registered unhappily with my limited build. The idea of receiving innumerable spheres of sodden leather to the tenderest part of my anatomy soon sent me in search of excuses to bow out.

I reverted to the great 'note from home' caper, the infamous piece of paper which appeared with regularity requesting that so-and-so be excused from any strenuous exercise. More often than not it was forged or simply re-used. Mine surfaced at an alarming rate, until my pathetic document of abstinence looked as I should have looked, had my complaints been genuine. Menial chores would be found for those choosing not to participate, a luxury unintentionally bestowed. Anything beat standing on a muddy pitch as the constant drizzle chilled you to the marrow, so while my classmates clashed like Titans in a fog-bank between two goalposts, I remained warm in the sports store applying linseed oil to cricket bats.

This was my first experience of narcotics, and as I applied the substance to a rag a heady feeling of euphoria overcame me. In a short time the limited space contained a haze of fumes that had nowhere to go but into my system. Ultimately I could be found singing away, happily surrounded by an array of mutilated jockstraps. I enjoyed the isolation of my tiny room and resented any help whatsoever, going so far as to say as much to the coach. Fearing that brain damage was imminent, he moved me to the equipment room at the rear of the main hall and it was here that one of my finest *faux pas* was executed. Before unfolding the details of this incident I should point out I was not unaided in my stupidity, for I had found a replacement for Peter Cale in the shape of one Danny Philips. Danny arrived in the spring of '62 and was also an Air Force offspring from the Woolworth base. From the moment of our introduction we became firm friends, remaining inseparable for the next five years. We each became aware that without the other's sense of the absurd to lean on, elements around us would stifle us with lead-footed oppression, and together we became happily intolerant of everyone and everything. Our union built one strong singular force that incorporated all our idiosyncrasies and dismissed our insecurities. Together, the mechanism of this educational asylum became tolerable and over the years we frequently turned calm into chaos.

Danny was tall, slender and athletic with an impish face and twinkling eyes that flashed above a mouthful of irregular teeth. On this particular occasion he was assisting me in the stacking of mats and medicine-balls. As we worked away amid the rising dust, chatting about nothing in particular, the somewhat unsteady silhouette of Mr Campbell appeared in the doorway. Mr Campbell was known to have a penchant for a few G & Ts during the lunch hour, which did little to enhance his already bulbous nose. Nicknamed 'Rudolph' for visually apparent reasons, he taught drama, music and religion. That day he looked particularly the worse for wear, a glazed look in his eyes accentuating his bloodshot pupils. His two narrow sockets appeared like luminous road maps in the dimly lit room. Beckoning us into the hall, he informed us in a slurred monotone that he had just taken possession of the new school piano and was enlisting us to remove the old one from the stage. Our heads bobbed from side to side attempting to avoid contact with the bombardment of alcoholic fire assailing our faces. At the conclusion of his request, I asked simply what he wished us to do with the old piano. With an incoherent shake of the head, he threw up his hands and said, 'I dunno, chop the bloody thing up if you want, just get rid of it.' Danny and I turned to each other with looks of disbelief. We had seen old Rudolph in various stages of pixilation, but this time he was really snockered! Not that this caused us any due concern, for we were too busy searching for implements of destruction.

Locating two large axes, we returned to the hall and took the back stairs up to the stage. There in the corner behind the curtain stood the piano. It was not at all the ole johana we had expected, and we both agreed it had been a rash expense to throw good money away when such a nice old piano still existed. However, it was not our place to question our superiors, and besides, how often did we get the chance legally to destroy school property? I brought my axe down, striking the first blow and causing the sickening sound of splintering rosewood to echo through the empty hall. For the next hour Danny and I worked up a sweat by reducing the once-fine old upright into a pile of kindling. Neatly we stacked the wood, swept up the splinters and boxed the hinges until space was made available for its replacement.

At assembly the next morning we gathered as usual for prayer and song. As the staff lined up solemnly on the stage, our pianist Miss Hall stepped towards the curtained corner to make her musical contribution. When she disappeared behind the curtains it was normally the cue to raise our hymnals and prepare to sing. Today that beat of anticipation continued, and a hush fell upon the congregation as Miss Hall backed out of the corner mouthing a silent scream as she pointed towards the curtains. The staff rushed to console her as each in turn moved towards the corner and peered into the recess; all except Mr Campbell who remained rooted to the spot, whistling through his teeth and staring into space. Danny and I glanced guiltily at each other with the distinct feeling that what was hidden from us today was the remains of what was once so prevalent yesterday. Assembly was dismissed and inquiries were made. Within the hour detection had unearthed the facts, and the verdict was out.

A new piano had been delivered but Mr Campbell, far from sobriety, had forgotten that before his liquid hiatus two other boys had been instructed to do the same thing he later had us do. These lads had removed the old piano and replaced it with the new one, so that when we arrived it was *chop chop* and *c'est la vie* new johana. When Miss Hall went to lay her fingers upon the new ivories she found nothing more than a neat stack of shiny firewood. There was little to blame us for except a certain lack of common sense and a little too much exuberance. The headmaster, being aware of Mr Campbell's habits, found the affair not too hard to swallow. We were exonerated and became minor celebrities, while Mr Campbell resigned when the effects of his obsession overtook the object of his reason.

Have you ever lived in a cage
where you live to be whipped and be tamed?

———————————

Like all young men embarking on their teenage years I was suddenly aware of the female form, realizing how pleasurable it was to the eye. Up to this point in adolescence I perceived all women as purely the materialistic possessions of men. They fed the furnace that brought home the bacon and tucked in the loose ends when the family felt shabby. Their domestic duties entailed a continuing service to the male species, who merely patted them on the bum and bought them a new dress every six months. I could be excused my opinion of woman's role in the world, for after all I was only twelve years old. Unfortunately my naive thinking is still shared by many men three times that age and upwards. My mother, of course, was excused from any derogatory associations, for like all good children I believed her to be the best in the world. She embodied the female role in our family with dignity and grace, executing the most menial tasks with a sense of pride. It's been said that no woman is as wise as your mother and none so loving, and in my case I believed it whole-heartedly.

When Pauline Barnes entered the dinner hall on her first day of school, I clutched at the shaft of Cupid's dart. Enthusiastically I related to Danny that this fresh-faced vixen had changed my life, and made my knees tremble and my heart skip to the beat of a different drum. She was unlike any girl I had ever seen, with an ethereal quality that seemed to make her float above her counterparts. Neat and well-groomed, she wore her pleated skirt and blouse as if they were a stole of ermine. I was painfully shy, an affliction definitely restricting my contact with girls. Every attempted approach resulted in my face turning the colour of fire. My tongue would tie itself in a double Windsor until the recipient of my advances became concerned for my health and not myself. With Pauline the campaign for conquest did not take long, and I was soon informed by the jungle telegraph that my feelings were reciprocated. Our courtship began and love's young bloom blossomed behind the library. For those of you expecting picturesque details of deflowerment at the inexperienced hands of yours truly, your time has yet to come, for lust never resulted in even the holding of hands. Pauline and I simply stared into each other's eyes, never daring to attempt the indecencies that my longing would have me do.

One reason for my lack of action was the ever-present shadow of her unattractive girlfriend. Totally insensitive to the meaning of privacy, she was continually shovelling vast amounts of crisps into a mouth resembling a Magimix. I always wondered what made reasonably pretty girls associate with bovine she-dragons and presumed it had something to do with non-competition. It always seemed that when a friend and I were faced with a female duo, it was the first to mutter, 'I don't think much of yours' who got the pick of the pair. This left your mate little choice but to remain inconspicuous, as anyone noticing the situation would be sure to comment, 'So you got the dog, aye?' Cruel but accurate, sympathy did not dwell in the hearts of randy teenagers. I shall never know if it was my lack of sexual innuendo that caused the inevitable split, but before long both sighs of relief and parting tears mingled in the afterglow, bidding a fond farewell to first love. Sometime later a rumour reached me that Pauline had been ravaged by a grammar school boy in the haystack of a nearby farm. This news shattered me completely, not because of love so recently lost but because I hadn't the guts to get there first.

In the aftermath of Pauline's deception I found myself associating more and more with the sad lyrical content of current ballads. There was something pleasantly masochistic about wallowing in the woes of unrequited love. Songs such as 'A Town Without Pity' and 'Crying in the Rain' enabled me to appear the hopeless romantic, crumbling beneath the burden of a broken heart. I wish that heartbreak for those truly suffering could be borne as easily as a child feels it in pretending.

My interest in pop music sometimes caused me to risk ridicule and embarrassment. At this time there were no periodicals dealing solely with the topic of rock. The only magazines carrying anything at all were the weekly schoolgirl rags, which usually allotted one page to titbits and pictures of the current stars, the remainder being cartoon strips full of romantic drivel. They had titles created to titillate the teenage fancy like *Boyfriend* and *Valentine*. On occasion I ventured to the post office in Doramby intent on securing a copy for myself to keep me enlightened, but the last thing I was about to do was hand over my sixpence and ask for *Boyfriend*, lest the entire village be informed that the Taupin kid was into 'The Loves of Diana Darling' and 'How to Crochet Tea Cosies'. Villages are incestuous places and word travels fast, so I was careful not to give rise to any vulgar humour pertaining to my masculinity. I would walk in wearing a perplexed frown and proceed to thumb through the recent tabloids, saying in a loud voice, 'Oh, bother! What was the name of that paper my *sister* wanted?' Gaining the shopkeeper's attention I would inquire, 'You know, that *dumb* girls' paper.' After effective guttural sounds of fake annoyance, he would name the object of my search as I concurred, 'That's the one. Next time my *sister* can get her own *dumb* magazine.' My prize secured, I would return home and retire to my room to paw over the condescending gossip from the world of showbiz.

My current hero was Joe Brown, a cockney guitarist with a disarming smile and a haircut like a blond floor-mop. Brown was far from hard-core, but his personality was endearing and he kept good company, dueting with the likes of Eddie Cochran and Gene Vincent. Dutifully I sent in my half-a-crown and was enrolled in his fan club. Joe was never one of the greats, and although he played his guitar behind his head long before Hendrix, his star never shone quite as brightly as those of the big three of Cliff, Billy and Adam.

Image was a constant attraction for me and I tended to be drawn by looks as much as music. Like Joe Brown, Billy Fury possessed tremendous charisma, and while Joe was chirpy and cheerful, Billy was mean and moody. With his lamé jackets and turned-up collars he was accused of emulating Elvis, but in many ways he was Britain's original punk. It was difficult to keep track of the more innovative American stars, and while I much preferred the barrel-house thunder of Jerry Lee Lewis and Little Richard, the English contingent did an admirable job of keeping the flag flying. Complacency still called the tune, but as the summer of '62 crawled to an end, the inner beast of beat stirred from slumber within the hollow dungeons of the northern towns. Soon the crest once dominated by Yankee power would feel the scorching fall-out of a working-class holocaust, and never again would rock and roll be regarded as a second-class citizen.

Four

On close scrutiny the bathroom mirror confirmed my worst fears. The new hairstyle I had begged the barber to create for me looked a lot like Henry V and not the slightest bit like George Harrison. I had gone into Market Slaten intent on having my hair styled to resemble that of the Beatle, only to have the barber ignore my request and basin-cut my hair into a sure match for Mo Howard.

I was in my third year at school when the advent of the Beatles heralded a revolution in fashion that set new trends in the way we all looked and thought. A year earlier they had invaded the media, outraging the old and endearing themselves to the young. They had been regarded by sects of die-hard rockers as a flash in the pan, but the hits kept coming and it became apparent that these Beatles were immune to critical repellent, and fast on their way to becoming an English institution. I welcomed their arrival like a breath of fresh air in the stale jungle of kitsch glamour, as I emulated their actions and sought out any items pertaining to my new heroes. My savings were spent on collarless jackets and my feet slipped into my first pair of Chelsea boots with a Cuban heel. Up to this point fashion had meant little to me, and over the next few years I shunted back and forth in both my dress code and musical tastes. However, nothing could deter me at that precise moment from wishing to be a clone of any of the four lovable mop-tops.

Pop fans have for ever been a fickle breed and I was no exception. Popularity spawns rejection and no matter how valid and inspirational an act may be, nothing is more damaging than success. Like others, I found it easy to let my adulation of the Beatles slip when the scruffy, devil-may-care attitude of the

Rolling Stones entered the scene. Their demeanour did further damage to the ever-widening barrier between the young and old as the beat generation came of age.

Let me get electric, put a silk suit on . . .

The Old House became a shrine as the walls upstairs sprouted montages of fan worship. Hundreds of glossy pics torn from the pages of *Pop Weekly*, *Fabulous* and *Rave* clung for dear life to the damp plaster. The popaholic in me increasingly craved more, and anyone with hair touching their ears and who played guitar could be guaranteed a spot on my wall. I knew the words to every song and at times performed them for any luckless soul lured in by Tizer and wine-gums. These impromptu sessions would be conducted from an old table top and backed by several of my embarrassed friends strumming tennis rackets and thumping paint tins. The effect was less than I anticipated and my exaggerated movements were always greeted by stifled giggles from my limited audience. A tuneless rendition of 'Stand by Me' accompanied by dull plunking and irregular clanging could hardly have been pleasing to the ears, but I gave it my all and awarded myself an 'E' for effort, not to mention a 'B' for balls.

School had become more tolerable and if it had any redeeming quality it was that it opened me up to other people. Danny remained my closest confidant and I sorely missed him when I returned home in the evenings. The weekends seemed to drag without his comic relief, and I found myself drifting into friendships with several of the village lads. None of them remained close for long, but their presence was appreciated and in their company I killed time.

The distinction of best pal was a fleeting title in those days. Loyalties switched rapidly and your best friend one day could be as distant as a star the following week. I should be anaemic today when I think of the blood spilled in the formation of the pacts we made. We were free with our promises and swift with our pocket knives, but nothing endured any longer than our interest span and tempers healed faster than scars. One boy who stood the test of time was Keith Proctor, a pleasant youth who seemingly remained unchanged as the years rolled by. I could chalk it up to country living but, studying the growth results of others from our era, it would appear our contemporaries have fared a little less well. While Keith remained a veritable Peter Pan, others ballooned into two-legged tubs of brown ale hurling darts in the local pub. Whether Keith, like Faust, had signed on the dotted line I'll never know, but one thing's for sure, he was good company and we enjoyed the summer of '63 with the unabashed abandon of young colts.

Keith's father owned a small dairy farm down a quiet lane at the far end of Doramby. It was a splendid playground with all manner of hiding places suitable for instantaneous enjoyment and our plans were usually hatched in the barn situated in the centre of the yard. This old building boasted a marvellous hayloft from which the entire farm could be surveyed, and from this vantage point we satiated our warrior spirit by picking sparrows off the telegraph wire with air rifles. Keith was a good shot but somewhat careless, and his irresponsible behaviour once got the better of him when he persuaded a friend to let him shoot an apple off his head. Either Keith's aim was not up to scratch or his target decided to retire at the wrong moment, for the pellet fell short, drilling a small hole in the boy's temple. While this incident shows little intelligence on Keith's part, it is far more sensible than allowing a thirteen-year-old boy to open fire on you. I too was far from blameless and my fascination for guns had me performing right alongside this would-be William Tell. We clocked up many hours sending a hail of pellets into the gum-boots of terrified youngsters as they made their way home along the drain ditch. Lying on the bank, we roared with laughter as they reacted to the stinging lead with screams for mercy. More often than not I got as good as I gave, and in one epic war marathon received the full force of a catapulted marble that tore through the skin on the bottom of my jaw, leaving me lying in a pool of blood. No sooner had I recovered than one of the boys whom Keith and I had tortured for so long with our sniping dropped a German bayonet from a great height into my right thigh. I flaunted my scars with true dramatic flair but came to the conclusion that although Keith and I shared a common bond with Walter Mitty, he had definite leanings towards Jonah. However, this did not deter me and we continued the summer in less dangerous pursuits.

It was an idyllic time and the long hot days gave way to cool evenings that found us lying in the buckwheat picking burrs out of our socks. The flames died in the cornfields, leaving a charred stubble for the plough and a home for the new seed, as bats fanned the evening air heralding the dusk and showing us the way home. Our pace quickened when we passed the abandoned cottages at the end of the lane. They stood empty and silent, and in the half-light of evening their hollow sadness threw ghostly shadows on the gardens gone to seed. The breeze played through the shattered glass causing an eerie tinkling that beckoned us to enter. Like Ulysses' sirens, the haunting sound tempted us to test our courage and bid us enter at our own peril. On occasion we ventured in among the twisted vegetation and peered apprehensively through the limbless doors. Musty smells and decay abounded within as a farm cat, its translucent eyes pinpointed in the inner darkness, hissed menacingly as she warned us that this was the property of the night and hers to hunt alone. Complying with her wishes we left hurriedly, our credibility more or less intact.

So much time was spent in the fields that each blade of grass became a familiar marker and the study of inanimate objects a pastime. As a child sprawled upon the ground you lie in a smaller world, and as the clouds roll by in a cool blue September sky, the eye focuses and the fingers ferret among that which surrounds you. I would peer into this other world as industrious insects in a hurry laboured with purpose bristling beneath their feet. In contrast I merely lay there prodding them with twigs, confusing their direction until they buried themselves in frustration. Life offered us so much time to waste, and when play wore thin, nothing compared with the comfort we found in the soft green turf. The world ached to change us but we held out; like the spider and the ant we felt the prod of a far bigger stick as our vacation ended and the corridors of learning called us back.

Living like a lusty flower, running through the grass for hours,
rolling through the hay like a puppy child.

Satiated from summer and fully immersed in rock's new age, my return to study was somewhat half-hearted. As I had expected the Beatles were on everyone's lips. I threaded my conkers and eavesdropped on the gossip, still preferring to keep my opinions to myself. Hopefully my refusal to join in these debates wasn't mistaken for a superior attitude, although in retrospect it just might have been. I was extremely protective of my thoughts and tended to guard my opinions, feeling that they belonged to me alone. It was the same way I had regarded my childhood novels and heroes, confident that I was the only one who truly understood the message. Only I knew the entrance to the 'Hundred Acre Wood' or the whereabouts of the streams where the stalwart Ratty punted the ever-petulant Mole. While my classmates were arguing whether Dave Clarke might capture the Beatles' crown or whether Mick Jagger was sexy or just plain ugly, I remained impartial, swinging my conker into the competition.

I continued to struggle in my schoolwork, remaining hopelessly stupid in anything remotely mathematical, but with Danny's help I managed to keep my head above water. With the onset of geometry and trigonometry, however, the taxation on my mind became unbearable and I sank like a stone. In fact my performance was so bad that the following year I was given up as a lost cause and offered an alternative class. What I lacked in mathematics I made up for admirably in English literature and language, and thoroughly enjoyed creating elaborate compositions that earned me glowing reports. My knowledge of poetry and prose was at last paying off and I went to great lengths to memorize many of the epics from the *Oxford Book of Verse*, standing in the kitchen reciting with my mother acting as prompter. In this manner I learned verbatim much of Macaulay's *Lays of Ancient Rome*, Coleridge's 'The Rime of the Ancient Mariner' and heaps of Tennyson, including 'The Charge of the Light Brigade' and 'Morte d'Arthur'. These, along with many others, became an obsession and the feeling I experienced from recitation gave me an unequalled sense of achievement. I may have burnt out in the field of equation, but I soared like a phoenix in literary exhibitionism.

Arriving around this time was a young teacher by the name of Mr Appleton, whose radical appearance endeared him to the student body. A would-be jazz buff, he had recently graduated from college and, deciding to work his way down, had consented to propel the rabble to a higher plain of learning. Something of a musical snob, when approached about rock and roll he would go to great lengths to dismiss it as infantile and disposable. The legacy of Charlie Parker and the free-form jazz fusion of Sun Ra were more to his liking. Needless to say he was fighting a losing battle, for expecting a thirteen-year-old to appreciate Thelonious Monk would be like asking Bing Crosby to sing 'Be Bop a Lu La'. Although later in my life jazz became a firm favourite, at the time it rated a big fat zero. Still, his heroes were more radical than Beethoven and you could usually depend on him for an interesting class.

In the spring of the following year Mr Appleton was put in charge of thirty students on a trip to Switzerland, and Danny and I were lucky enough to be included. Barely able to contain ourselves, we slept restlessly for days before our departure and on a cold April morning in 1964 set forth to shatter the tranquillity of the Swiss Alps. After taking the early-morning train from Lincoln to King's Cross, we boarded another which reached Dover later in the day. None of us had experienced a hovercraft before, and after a sickening hour from Dover to Calais we stumbled on to foreign turf looking green and nauseous. The warm carbonated drinks and fish-paste sandwiches we had devoured on the train disagreed with the choppy waters of the English Channel, and by the time we reached Calais we were ready to 'heave ho' our hearts. Once through customs we were herded on to yet another train which hurtled through France and Austria, depositing us in the small mountain village of Wilderswil. By the time we arrived at the hotel our spirits had picked up. With the cruel sea virtually forgotten, Danny and I immediately set to the task of short-sheeting beds, raiding the kitchen and locating Linda Darnely's room.

Linda was a fabulous strumpet, the school tease and an all-round tart. The discovery of her room and the access of the keyhole would give us a divine door through which to view the pleasures of the flesh. Unfortunately by the time we arrived there was a line forming down the hallway. Discretion taking second place to obsession, we grudgingly tagged on behind. Finally we made it and, as we leaned in towards our feast, Linda Darnely turned out the light and Mr Appleton booted us in the behind. That first night we retired sore of rear, our pornographic thirst unquenched.

49

Wilderswil was a charming village nestling at the foot of the spectacular mountains of the Jungfrau region. Like a picture postcard, it oozed cuckoo clocks and lederhosen. Rustic chalets lined the streets and tiny farms were scattered across the hillside like so many wooden boxes. Sheep bleated and cattle lowed as the echoing sounds of their hollow bells rang through the valley. We were close to the popular ski resort of Interlaken, and over thirty miles from the capital city of Bern. Everywhere we went the people seemed gentle and shy and showed no outward resentment at an influx from the outside world. Of course, we did little to convey the same traits and went to extremes to prove ourselves unworthy ambassadors of Great Britain. At one point we staged a massive booze-up in the local *Beerkeller*. After numerous litres and just as many visits to the toilet, we realized we were being served non-alcoholic beer. We shouldn't have been surprised, for we were well below drinking age and looked it, but it was as close as we were going to get and we did our best to fake inebriation. Hurling our arms around each other, Danny and I stumbled through the quiet village streets yodelling at the top of our lungs.

Once we did manage to steal half a bottle of schnapps from the hotel bar and, retiring to our room, proceeded to get plastered. This episode ended with Danny falling out the window as he reached for an apple in a nearby tree. One minute he was sitting on the sill groping the night air; the next thing I knew, he was gone. We found him half an hour later cradled in a myrtle bush singing 'Swiss Maid', quite oblivious to his predicament.

There were moments among the madness when points of geological interest did make an impression on us. We explored caves of stalagmites and stalactites and witnessed giant underground waterfalls that roared down the mountainside arcing and swooping through caverns of smooth marble-like rock. Sculptured by endless torrents of foam, their flow had not ceased since the dawn of creation, and they drowned all sound with their thunderous voices, leaving us gasping in wonder as the chilly waters washed over us in a fine mist. In general, although we made many excursions to places of historic interest, little lodged in our memory longer than it took to eat an ice-cream and purchase a cheap souvenir. Our time on the slopes was normally spent in a jealous huddle, muttering racial slurs directed at the skiing skills of Aryan Adonises as they sliced gracefully through the snow. The approving squeals of our female companions only irritated our Lincolnshire machismo, and sour grapes accentuated our idiocy, making us appear exactly what we were: a bunch of clod-hopping plough-boys stumbling around as Germanic supremacy showed us the way.

We found the ski lifts tremendous fun and took pleasure in rocking them violently upon discovering Mr Appleton's phobia for heights. The greener he became, the harder we swung and, not wishing his fear to become apparent, he clung desperately to the edge staring wildly into space, his hand clamped tightly over his mouth. Once at the peak, Mr Appleton headed to the washroom while we immediately involved ourselves in a snowball war culminating in the complete annihilation of our giggling counterparts. As dusk approached the sun fell in slow motion, its colours creating a contrast of luminous shadows that swept the Alps, calming our wild spirits for a whispered moment. In that instant we were drawn together by a common bond as fleeting as a sigh, for no sooner had it begun than it was shattered by a bell indicating the last lift into the valley. After hesitating for one last look, I turned and joined the screaming horde which had now returned to heathen proportions. In a daze I dreamed I might some day see mountains of different nations, and as the sun sank slowly in the west, I snapped out of my trance and followed Linda Darnely's swaying buttocks into the mist.

> *. . . like flags of many nations*
> *flying high above her head.*

I guess most kids at one time or another have a paper round and I was no exception. In order to pocket some extra money I took to delivering the *Lincolnshire Echo*. The papers arrived on the five o'clock bus and I picked them up at Eric Beaton's house on the outskirts of the village. Eric delivered the dailies but decided it was to his advantage to use child labour for the evening stint. There were about fifty papers on average and, considering the time element involved, it wasn't unpleasant employment. On top of my wage, it was possible to make several tips on a Friday night, depending on whom you could catch in a good mood at the end of the working week. During the winter months the job was far less agreeable, and pedalling uphill against the driving wind or being pursued by a bad-tempered dog was no picnic. The icy roads often left me lying on my back looking at the stars, and there were times when I found it necessary to abandon my bike altogether and make my deliveries on foot. After a while I tended to get erratic in my rounds and on several occasions was roasted for delivering papers to the wrong addresses. This was no doubt due to my mind wandering off to places unknown and, given the monotony of the routine, it was easy to set one's mind on automatic pilot and cruise through the deliveries.

Once, in the depth of a particularly nasty January, my paper round clashed with an extremely tempting offer made by Keith Proctor. He had hinted at the terrific prospects of an evening's rabbiting in the fields adjacent to his father's property. This was the kind of thing I loved to do and the idea of crunching through the crisp snow in search of our quarry was most appealing. The problem was that in order to catch our prey at peak time it was necessary to begin before six; the light of the moon on the snow making it easier to spot the rabbits. If I had to do my paper round I wouldn't finish in time, and in desperation I devised a plan to remove this obstacle from my path.

Due to the weather, bad road conditions occasionally made it impossible for the buses to maintain their correct schedule and from time to time the delivery of the papers would be cancelled. On this night I was about to scrap the delivery whether it arrived or not. Racing down to Eric's house I met the bus and collected the papers. Luckily Eric never followed the patterns of public transport, so whether the bus arrived or not he was none the wiser. Rushing back to my house I grabbed a bottle of paraffin and a box of matches and crept into our field where I found a secluded corner, doused the papers and threw a match on them. Satisfied with the fire, I turned and left, presuming the flames would do the correct thing and destroy the evidence. Tomorrow I would tell Eric that due to the weather no papers had arrived the night before. I was a desperate man and oblivious to the cards stacked against me. I would simply explain to our subscribers that a minor hitch had put a temporary dent in the news service. No problem, it was a cut-and-dried situation and, the deed done, I ran off to join Keith for an evening in the fields.

All would have gone according to plan had the wind not decided to kick up a fuss, and that night when I returned from the hunt it was creating havoc among the trees. The next day when I left home to catch the school bus, I noticed a scowl on the faces of many who normally greeted me with a cheery 'good morning'. Putting this frosty reception down to the weather, I continued with my day and on returning that evening jumped on my bike and rode down to Eric's to do my rounds. From a distance I could see that my employer was on hand and I detected something was amiss. Normally he was nowhere to be seen, but this evening he was pacing up and down the curb with an agitated look on his face. As I came closer I could see he was clutching what looked, to my dismay, like a handful of charred newspapers. Before I had a chance to open my mouth, he thrust them under my nose and demanded an explanation. I had none and all I could do was feign ignorance in the face of accusation.

Early that morning the villagers had drawn their curtains to find scraps of singed newspaper stuck all over their windows. On closer examination they noticed the date on some of the pieces was yesterday's, and it didn't take a genius to realize that the soggy scraps they held were particles of the papers they should have received the night before. What I hadn't taken into account was that the flames had been extinguished by the wind long before they had a chance to complete the job, and consequently the remains were scattered to all four corners of the village. All this became apparent to me as I stood averting my eyes from Eric's accusatory stare. There wasn't a lot I could say and it was obvious I'd sacrificed my job. Yesterday's news had refused to go unread and had risen from the ashes to confront me with my folly.

> *. . . get a little headline news.*
> *I'd like to see what the papers say*
> *on the state of teenage blues.*

By now I was fourteen and thought the Animals' 'House of the Rising Sun' was the greatest thing I'd ever heard. I was also becoming increasingly aware of my randiness. Not that this discovery served me well as I was still very much at the window-shopping stage. We colonials of the Sixties were no match for our city-dwelling counterparts and not even close to the standards set by today's youth. Now it seems that kids are into group sex and bisexuality at an age when I thought a bisexual was something you rode to school on. There were the obvious crushes I harboured in my heart, but for me the pleasures of the flesh had to wait along with my yearning desire to communicate. There was the normal schoolboy titillation resulting from well-thumbed copies of *Parade*, while literate pornography came with the more educated pervert clutching *Lady Chatterley's Lover* and *Fanny Hill*, their juciest pages turned back for rapid access. This was all very exciting, but I tended to associate lust and fornication with toilets and the dark corners of bicycle sheds. Needless to say, my interest in sex was as keen as everyone else's and I was just as eager to learn how to obtain the pleasures of the flesh at first hand. Actually, it was my right hand, and remains so, unless a shift in my body chemistry decides otherwise. From the moment the connection was made between the thrill of the picture and the pleasure in my palm, nothing could deter me from my discovery. If this was truly the path to blindness, then I was happy to stumble through the future supported by a thin white cane.

It was at around this time that our school was visited by one of its favourite sons. I remember this well, for it amazed me the lengths to which the school board would go to find an ex-student worth honouring. Bill Dale had been in his last year when I was in my first, and the quality my classmates and I best remembered about him was that he was without a doubt the most merciless bully any of us could recall. His sheer brutality and his torture of those smaller than he were legendary, and how this lethargic diplodocus had amounted to anything worthy of esteem was beyond us. However, the simple fact that he had joined the Marines and made Seaman Second Class was enough to send the teaching staff into ecstasy. To them this was an achievement of great magnitude and we were herded into assembly to pay homage to this naval numbnuts. There the staff treated us to a treacle-laden speech full of pompous talk on the gratification of hard work, through which Dale stood smugly to one side scratching his balls. To add insult to injury, Dale imparted several pearls of wisdom to the effect that it was a man's life on the seven seas, sailing far and wide to exotic places. Personally I doubted if he had ever sailed north of the Humber and imagined he spent most of his time with a mop in his hands. He impressed very few of us, as many of those assembled recalled his wrath all too vividly, and it was the general desire that his attitude might get him gangbanged by the entire fleet. I chalk this incident up to despair. Any achievement, no matter how small, was received with such adulation that even a calculated bully became a hero in the eyes of long-suffering adults. Little of this animosity was ripe in my soul back then, and it meant more to me to cultivate my interests. I wasn't fickle, but there was something in me that tended to enjoy things for a short spell, lose interest rapidly and soon forget they were ever a part of my life. First, there were the rabbits.

It all started when the man who delivered chicken feed to our farm gave me a small brown rabbit. I immediately foresaw in my future a rabbit empire with this bunny as its charter member. Within the hour I had spread out several bales of hay on the floor of my room in the Old House and set down water-feeders and bowls of pellets. Over the next week I acquired several more rabbits and by the end of the month the total was up to eight. Unfortunately as my empire grew my enthusiasm waned, and despite the beauty of my angoras, chinchillas and Dutches, all I saw was the task of cleaning and feeding. Whether it was my lack of interest or the fact that they just lost the will to live I'll never know, but I found them all stiff as boards one morning. I was visibly shocked if not a little relieved, as they had become a burden to me. However, I felt that mass suicide was quite unnecessary and, with a heavy heart, I wrapped them in the straw in which they had died and buried them in the open field. A sad end but a necessity for my Alamo Museum.

I have always had a fascination for deeds of great valour, from my play-acting in the role of Horatius to my plastic facsimiles re-enacting Rorke's Drift. None, though, had captured my imagination more than the thirteen days of glory at the siege of the Alamo. I had a passion for the rugged period from the opening of the West until the late 1800s, and its romance and lawlessness intrigued me. Westerns were a staple diet and when the big-screen version of John Wayne's *The Alamo* hit the ABC in Lincoln, the bug bit deeper than ever before. It was one of my more imaginative endeavours as I transformed my faithful old room into a replica of the infamous San Antonio Mission. I placed crates and tables along the walls, on which I piled a collection of historic artefacts from the legendary battle. A broken kitchen knife became the remains of Bowie's famous blade and the torn remnants of an old fur coat Davy Crockett's coonskin cap. I was considering using a dead cat, but even I couldn't handle anything that close to reality. Breeze-blocks became bricks from the battlements, rusty pennies medals from Travis's uniform, and railing spikes were Mexican lance-heads. Everything was liberally doused with ketchup to give the necessary effect of gory victory. There was an entrance fee to this feast of Americana, a fee – I might add – that my mother paid continually without complaint, she being my only patron of the arts. Ultimately, like the Alamo itself, so did my own fort fall; the original to the Mexicans, mine to boredom.

Five

Never flagging in attempts to amuse myself, I more often than not dragged into my inventive web anyone willing to participate in the Frankensteins I invariably created. So it was that around the time my museum closed its doors to business, I nearly poisoned Piggy Sharpe, decapitated David Payne and blew all three of us to kingdom come.

David Payne was several years younger than I and rather anaemic due to occasional bouts of asthma. Piggy Sharpe, on the other hand, was built like a plough-horse, and moved and thought like a plough-horse. The day started pleasantly enough with an excursion to a tiny stream on the edge of the Todmoor where, like true adventurers, we set up camp on the soggy turf. The field had a terrible drainage problem which made pitching our tent an ordeal, for no sooner had we set our poles on one side than the other side would sink, leaving us about three feet of canvas to crawl under. While mud oozed through the many holes in our groundsheet, we unpacked our gear and set up our Primus stove with every intention of frying up the 'catch of the day'.

With our encampment perched precariously on the unsteady terrain, we made our way down the embankment, fishing nets firmly in hand. What we intended to land is still a mystery to me. Save the odd stickleback and minnow, I'm unaware of any fish that can survive in three inches of dank pond water but, undaunted to a man, we sat and waited patiently for the big one. Surely it was only a matter of time until the legendary Old Gentleman of the Beck would be furiously entangled in the thin mesh of my trusty bamboo net. As the gnats and midges buzzed around us feeding heartily on tender young flesh, we stared blankly into the water willing whatever lay beneath to venture forth and be taken.

It was a glorious morning, of the kind that makes country living everything it's cracked up to be. Large unruly hedges arced over the stream, forming dark mysterious tunnels of vegetation above the tranquil water lapping against the rocks. Upstream the occasional moorhen bobbed for breakfast as martins swooped from the sky, landing in the branches above us to rip off the rosehips and return with them to the new-born. Up the slope on the far side of the stream, cattle roamed among the tall grass, tearing up the tender new shoots that sprang irrepressibly from the sunlit hill. This serenity was rudely broken when Piggy's characteristic snort brought me instantly back to the order of the day. He was on his knees peering into his net, excited by its contents.

'What the bloody 'ell's these things?' he asked.

'Shrimps,' I replied knowledgeably.

'Lunch!' we all chimed in unison.

Out came the frying pan and on went the Primus as Piggy proudly displayed his catch.

I think it was at this moment that the penny dropped. I was no angling wizard but it didn't take a biologist to realize that edible shrimps were not habitually found in country streams and ponds. What Piggy had snared was a form of fresh-water shrimp – totally inedible and highly contaminated, definitely not the 'dunk 'em in cocktail sauce' type. The problem was, did I go back on my initial opinion and admit my mistake, or rely on Piggy's cast-iron stomach to digest these minute grey crustaceans? Discretion, valour and any other virtue I might have possessed at the time were thrown to the wind. I feigned a loss of appetite for David and myself and returned to the stream, leaving Piggy happily sautéing his catch over the open flame. David was a little perturbed that I had dragged him away from lunch, but I managed to cover myself with references to bigger and better things.

It was not fifteen minutes later that we heard the distant sound of retching and strangled cries for help. Leaping to our feet, we ran back to our ailing comrade. Guilt welled up inside me as my conscience screamed 'murderer' - a death on my hands and a blot on the family name were more than I could bear! Before us on all fours was Piggy, green and puking, his bulk heaving forth the poisonous contents of his stomach. He reminded me of a large, pathetic hound that has consumed too much greenery and retches uncontrollably on the front lawn. I cursed my insensitivity as I felt I was totally to blame for my friend's condition. Administering first-aid was not easy, for Piggy was in the dry-heaving stage and becoming erratic in his gestures of displeasure. Not wishing to get in the way, we offered him a bottle of luke-warm Cherryade and gingerly stepped out of range. The danger soon passed and, much to my relief, he recovered rapidly. 'Off the hook,' I thought, no pun intended. Turning towards us with a look of disgust, he wiped his mouth with the back of his hand and said, 'Bleedin' shrimps was awful!'

After this incident it was unanimously decided to curtail our fishing trip and instead explore the cricket pavilion in the next field. A mainstay of most local sportsgrounds, the pavilion was the nerve centre of provincial competition. From these structures of white-washed clapboard the kitted batsman strode forth to meet his adversary, while the clump of spikes resounded from within as the players padded up and prepared to do battle. Now it lay silent, the ghosts of the weekend murmuring in the creaking walls as the smell of linseed mingled with pungent stabs of honest sweat. We found the pavilion an exciting place, its confined space housing the standard props essential to the game, including the scorebook detailing the teams' triumphs and defeats. The keeping of this bible of facts and figures was the duty of a crusty old soul called Smitty. Each weekend he hunched over its yellowed pages, puffing a Woodbine under the brim of a beaten trilby, grunting out the score to his assistant. Diligently the lad replaced the numbered metal squares to inform the scattered crowd of the game's progress. Now these markers littered the ground about our feet, their paint chipped, their hanging holes stretched by years of tugging on rusty nails.

My favourite aspect of country cricket had little to do with the game and more to do with my stomach. Stacked neatly in the corner were the trestles on which the half-time tea was laid. With bustling efficiency, the village women prepared mountains of freshly cut sandwiches and steaming pots of tea. I would sit close and watch with envy as the players tucked into chopped egg and cucumber, and cheese and tomato, laid between thin slices of soft white bread. Little carpets of cress lay neatly on white doilies surrounding crusty sausage rolls, as angels on horseback liberally sprinkled with powdered sugar melted, to my annoyance, in the mouths of others. The most we ever got if we could come up with sixpence was a solidifying leftover and a glass of tepid orange juice. All things considered, there was something very appetizing about this weekly event, the sun reflecting off white flannel, the smack of the ball whistling down centre-field and the ceaseless drone of insects annoying picnickers in the outfield. It really wasn't so much the game as the sense of occasion and the community spirit involved. Lying on a blanket in the shade of a willow whittling a briar stalk might sound like a Constable canvas, but it was real life, more like the Archers – 'an everyday story of country folk'.

I was daydreaming and probably salivating over the visions of pasties and pastries when David's cry of joy broke the silence. He had discovered a set of golf clubs behind a bundle of umpires' coats, a little rusty and the worse for wear, but definitely the honest-to-goodness Arnold Palmer gear. None of us had ever wielded one of these impressive implements and we dragged them on to the field squabbling incessantly over who was to have first whack. Brawn would have won over brains and Piggy would have taken the initial stroke, but right now old Pig was still feeling queasy after his 'shrimp à la pond' and we decided to let David take the first stroke. Digging out the pitted excuse for a ball, we aligned it with precision on the nearest mole hill and prepared to tee off. We soon found it was far more difficult than it appeared on the telly and before long were all extremely irritable; first, with the impossible act of making contact with the ball, and ultimately with ourselves for failing to make an impression on each other. No amount of hacking and slicing could unseat the ball from its position, although Piggy came the closest, missing the ball by inches and managing to propel a nearby dog turd into orbit. Our behaviour became more erratic and our swinging less thoughtful as, fuelled by aggression, we lashed at the leering ball with venom. In a fit of blind fury I grabbed the driver from David and pushed him behind me, vowing that this time the ball was bound for outer space. I swung back with full force, forgetting David was right behind me. Contact was made! Unfortunately it was with a resounding thud directly behind me, followed instantly by one directly below me. The club remained frozen in its swing, shuddering from the connection that had felled my friend like a helpless tree. Spread-eagled on the ground, David Payne lay lifeless, his eyes rolled towards the heavens. 'Oh, Christ,' I thought, 'at this rate I'll end up knocking off the entire adolescent population of the village.' Numbed with shock Piggy and I stared at each other, mouths agape in silence until the eloquent Piggy blurted out accusingly, 'Bugger me, you've killed him!'

For the second time that day the hair on the back of my neck bristled, while the breakfast in my bowels jostled for release. I truly believed in that frozen moment that I had 'offed' my friend, a thought confirmed by the cold eyes of Piggy Sharpe as they pierced a passageway to my guilty soul. I felt the eyes of every surrounding insect and animal staring at me with accusation. 'I saw him die, said the spider to the fly.' In an eternal instant and in the space of time it would have taken Piggy to make a citizen's arrest, David's body shuddered, his eyes fluttered and he groaned. In true form Piggy spluttered, 'Bugger me, he's alive!' Promising to lay off the sacristy wine and say an extra set of Hail Marys for the next ten years, I fell to my knees beside David. In true Hardy and Nelson fashion I cradled his head in my hands, inquiring about his well-being. Thank God for a dull club! A sharp edge and I could have sent the top of his head sailing between the goal posts at the end of the field. David's focus began to clear along with my conscience, and before long even the cloud of paranoia above my head began to disperse. Soon all that was left of the incident was some tell-tale blood on the club and a welt on David's forehead.

Since both fishing and golfing were putting severe strains on our friendship, I suggested we return to the Old House to plan the remainder of the day. We walked the long mile home in stony silence, something that may have had a tranquillizing effect on my comrades, for by the time we hit the ridge bringing Bramby into view their spirits seemed rekindled and they began to laugh about their close brushes with death. In days to come they would get plenty of mileage out of these incidents, and I could hear the quadrangle hum with their desperate deeds at the hands of the grim reaper. I forgave them their impending white lies; after all, had it been me the details would have been romanticized beyond the boundaries of belief. Exaggeration being a horse, I rode at full gallop.

After some deliberation we decided to explore the section of the Old House once occupied by Mrs Peel, the old crone having moved on to the great coven in the sky. The thought of stepping across her threshold alone would never have crossed my mind. My part of the Old House was familiar and friendly, but I imagined a horde of hexes and curses awaiting anyone who dared to desecrate her inner sanctum. Up to this point the only time I had entered was on the tail of my father's coat, a cringing child gripping tight to a familiar thigh. Now, at an age when adventure beckoned and two slightly dubious friends stood by my side, I could laugh in the face of danger and toss suspicion to the winds – almost!

I mentioned earlier that Mrs Peel kept a pantry stacked with an amazing array of pots and bottles containing liquids and potions of varying colours and consistencies. I found these mesmerizing, for they conjured up images of late nights in the laboratory. To find out whether or not these brews were herbal, medicinal or alcoholic was the quest at hand. The mystery was the magic of the moment and, with the burning desire of discovery pounding in our hearts, we pushed open the door and stepped into the dank hallway. The walls and ceilings sagged, giving the entire dwelling a distorted appearance as if it were a misshapen relic tired of life, clinging as if on its last legs and threatening to let go at the slightest hint of release. The door closing behind us tore small tracer-lines in the plaster around the frame, causing little rivers of dust and mortar to trickle to the floor. The boards beneath our feet creaked without restraint like the bones of their former occupant, brittle and uneven. Aside from a bundle of *Daily Mirror*s dating back to a time before we were born, little remained in the neglected rooms: the odd roll of musty wallpaper, several scattered bedsprings and a shredded wicker chair long since dismantled by hungry rats. However, none of these things hampered the beeline we made for the back pantry and here, behind a heavy door, we located our witch's brewery.

Nothing in the room had been touched, and dust and cobwebs lay heavily on the bottles lining the shelves. Setting to the task at hand, we began inspecting each one individually, kicking up a minor dust-storm in the process. They were indeed labelled, but the years had not been kind and the ink had long since faded, leaving little to inform us of their contents. The most fascinating aspects were the colours and, as the dust settled, thin shafts of light breaking through a small vented window reflected their true hue. There were exotic ambers and emerald greens, purples and ruby reds, pure liquid jewellery sparkling in the surrounding decay. After some time in the pursuit of identifying these concoctions, a mask of boredom descended upon the faces of my friends and I sensed it was time to conjure up some remedy to keep the lads amused. My solution appeared entertaining as an idea, but potentially lethal in reality, as my capacity for logical conduct was becoming limited. In a final attempt to save the day I suggested we construct a Molotov cocktail from the selection of bottles at our disposal. All we needed was a rag, a match and a target. The prospect of the impending mayhem seemed to excite my two companions, proving that inside every small boy there lurks a potential arsonist. The rudimentary Molotov should be of gasoline content, a smell with which I was familiar, and although none of these liquids smelled remotely like petrol, I was confident there must be something of a combustible nature among these potions. By means of this experiment it would be possible to ascertain whether the contents were flammable or not, thus proving that our ingenuity went further than our sense of smell.

David was dispatched to locate a suitable piece of rag, while Piggy and I picked out a selection of the bottles we thought would make the best incendiary devices. David returned with an adequate piece of sacking and we began tearing it into strips to make wicks that would be secured tightly into the necks of the bottles. Our plan was that once the bombs were completed, we would take them to the rear of the house and hurl them into an area where there was little danger of igniting the surrounding foliage. Before venturing forth with our weaponry, we decided to test the matches I'd retrieved from our ill-fated fishing trip. Still damp from my soggy pocket, they spluttered helplessly as one by one they refused to ignite. Impatiently I flung them to the ground until the procedure became automatic. Rip, strike, splutter, toss. Rip, strike, splutter, toss. A hypnotic procedure broken only by Piggy's shriek of 'Bugger me, it's burnin'!' In my trance-like haste to find a dry match I had hurled aside a naked flame which had attached itself greedily to one of our makeshift fuses. The three of us leapt around, moronically mouthing 'oohs' and 'ahhs', fanning our hands furiously over the rapidly diminishing fuse. Picking up the bottle, I blew on it in vain until my cheeks ached and turned purple. I snatched at the wick and burned my fingers in an attempt to dislodge it, as the bottle became the round black bomb in a silent movie and David, Piggy and myself the Three Stooges doing our routine.

'Here, you take it!'

'I don't want it, you take it!'

'Bugger off, you lit it!'

A fraction of a second before our impending Armageddon I thought, 'What the hell!', turned and hurled the bottle into the pantry, closing the door. The instant the bomb had left my grip I remembered the scores of bottles within and, turning to my friends with a weak smile and a voice octaves higher than normal, commanded them to 'HIT THE DECK!'

I expected to hear a deafening explosion from within, but what emitted instead was a low rumble followed by a giant belch. As the tremor subsided, I realized the communication between my brain and body had malfunctioned. I was not lying face down on the floor with my friends, but was flattened against the pantry door with a death grip on the handle, only the handle was no longer attached to the door but now sat like an amputated limb in my palm. The uncomfortable silence was broken by a loud creaking as the door fell back off its hinges and crashed into the pantry below. The house was immediately filled with a sickeningly sweet smell. There was no doubt in my mind as I moved down the steps like a zombie to survey the damage that the cocktail had been made with the correct ingredients. The pantry was entirely gutted, with glass and liquid strewn about in murals no modern artist could ever dream of, and a smell of concentrated cologne hanging like a cloud in the air. It appeared that Mrs Peel was attempting to rival Max Factor rather than the black arts, and if the explosive nature of her creation was anything to go by, the wearer of this perfume would be potentially lethal in the fires of passion.

Shell-shocked and holding their noses, Piggy and David staggered through the smoking doorway. They stared into the crater I had created, and there was no point in contesting their opinion of me at that moment as I confronted their accusing eyes. Needless to say, neither of them spoke to me again, but as they turned the corner at the end of the street on that fateful day, I swear I heard Piggy say, 'That bugger's crazy!'

It took me some time to overcome the shock of my terrorist activities and a great deal longer to clean them up. At school I reneged on my classes in woodwork and metal-shop in order to stay well clear of the lathe and torch, and settled for the quiet life of domestic science, another pompous secondary school term that meant keeping house. I did not enrol in this class with the intention of pushing a broom but of taking up the extremely continental art of cuisine, and so it was that, surrounded by the cream of fourth-year beauty, I began to take cookery lessons.

I didn't encounter too much harassment or ridicule from my classmates for assigning myself to this activity; in fact, I think they admired me for having the guts to do it. The well-equipped modern structure in which we worked was a far cry from the draughty machine shop with its choking layers of dust and shavings. It was a warm environment where I was coached in a friendly atmosphere by a kindly old girl who seemed mildly amused and ultimately impressed by my enthusiasm. A bevy of giggling females jockeyed for the position of partnering me in the many projects assigned to us. They were not fighting for my affections but purely for the novelty of cooking beside yours truly in an apron. A cheap price to pay for recognition. I must say I enjoyed the attention and it made me realize that sometimes you have to take a chance in order to make life a little more interesting. I went into this blind to the fact that in my environment it was not acceptable for a man to make dinner. My life had become a slow-burning fuse willing itself to ignite rather than fizzle out unnoticed and unfulfilled. I wanted to shine if possible, and in time if my obsessions got the better of me then at least I could say there were moments in my life when I burned with a lovely light. Eliminating woodwork and adopting cookery was a minor move but a foothold worth fighting for and a step in the right direction.

School had taken a turn for the better. The fourth year made us senior students and with that came a position of power. This was also the year I was asked to retire from mathematics as my dishevelled and twitching teacher Miss Deery had come to the end of her tether with me. Biting her nails and running her hand through her greying thatch, she nervously asked me if I would not be happier elsewhere. She found it hard to believe that a fourteen-year-old boy could still fail to add and subtract correctly, and from then on my maths period was spent reading George Orwell and H. G. Wells in the school library.

This year also saw a vast improvement in my gymnastic skills, thanks in part to the encouragement of Danny. I was ultimately made the captain of my house team and became surprisingly athletic for a short period of time. I threw myself whole-heartedly into any amount of sporting activities ranging from five-aside football to badminton. Throughout all this Danny and I stretched ourselves to new heights of thoroughly dishonourable conduct and would wander aimlessly through the streets of Market Slaten during lunch break, squandering our dinner money on fish and chips and cigarettes. Occasionally we would harass a first-former or two by masquerading as prefects and demand to see the child's note of consent to walk the streets. We would question its authenticity until the quaking boy offered us a boiled sweet or some other sufficient bribe. We never intended to be bullies and always conducted ourselves with a great deal of humour and self-mockery. We never inflicted any hurt or caused pain, the memory of our own first years still fresh in our minds.

Are there chances in life for little Dirt Cowboys?

———————

Ever since our move to Bramby my parents had maintained a close connection with the Catholic church in Market Slaten, attending Mass every Sunday and on all Holy Days of Obligation. They were good Christians and by no means fanatical in their belief, but a little of the spark went out of it when it was decreed that the Latin Mass be dropped for a simpler approach. They had been partial to the old ways and they saw this change as rather distasteful, for in one fell swoop the Vatican had buried a legacy that had sat well with generations of Catholics. Tradition had deviated into a whitewashed format, leaving the beauty of High Mass to gather dust in the cloisters of so many houses of worship. Although my parents continued to attend after the axe fell, there were those among the congregation who saw the new Mass as Satan sitting in the pocket of the Pope. In particular there were a couple of spinsters from Middle Slaten who up to then had been the backbone of all things pertaining to the church. Dutifully dressed in sombre attire and clutching their missals to their ample bosoms, they attended with unflagging regularity. Pleasant in their piety, they could always afford a cheery smile as they entered the lich-gate that led down the leafy pathway to the portals of the church. They seemed content in their devotions, but when *Dominus vobiscum* fell dead on the lips of a thousand priests it was more than they could stand. They boycotted the church and encouraged all parishioners to do the same, becoming radical to the point where my father found it necessary to run for cover whenever they approached. They would bend ears unmercifully with talk of the destruction of sanctity and the desecration of the word of God. I pictured the two of them forming an élite corps of disgruntled grannies waylaying unsuspecting priests and press-ganging them into performing the old Mass.

Before this unfavourable change I had served with my brother in the somewhat unenthusiastic apprenticeship of altar boy. I don't recall how it all started but I'm certain it was not a duty I accepted out of choice, and can only assume it was a decision made for me. I recall at an early age being asked, 'Who made you?' as the Catechism was pumped into my idle mind. On Sunday afternoons that little red book was dragged out as we were orally examined on the origin of our species according to the Almighty. It seemed confusing – on one hand religion informed us that in a puff of smoke and a snap of celestial fingers man was created, while on the other history recorded our forefathers as lumbering apes lolloping across the tundra clubbing dinosaurs with tree trunks. The idea of an athletic Adam was more appealing, and the ideological presence of the Lord as my shepherd comforted me in my lamb-like childhood. At the time, the station of altar boy was regarded as a privileged position, but aside from the occasional tipple of sacristy wine, I don't ever remember seeing it that way. Arriving at the church, we would bustle back to the sacristy and don our robes, which in my case were consistently a size too small, elevating the hem of my garment several inches above my ankles and cutting off the circulation in my armpits. The overall effect of this tourniquet to my upper torso was to force me to raise my arms and hunch my shoulders in order to breathe. Anyone viewing this from the congregation might have mistaken me for a performing chimpanzee as I scuttled up and down the steps before the altar. I continually forgot my lines, never spoke loud enough and invariably fell asleep during the sermon. My brother, on the contrary, was the model of efficiency, having the entire proceedings very much in hand, but there was an occasion one Christmas when his conduct unbecoming put me to shame.

It was a tradition in our family to attend Midnight Mass on Christmas Eve and return home for a late supper and bed. Whether it was due to the expectation of presents or just seasonal goodwill, it was the one religious gathering of the year that I loved. The little church was always packed and the spirit of Christmas warmed the normally chilly interior, while outside the night was crisp and clear as our breath hung like soft white clouds in the evening air. The same stars that thousands of years ago had led the Three Wise Men to the manger of Christ shone with magnitude from the heavens above. Christmas brought the human experience into true proportion and allowed us all to view each other through rose-coloured glasses. For me Christmas Eve was a far more exciting occasion than Christmas Day; a happy evening tied together by the knots that bound our family with love. Sleepily we retired to warm beds with heads full of anticipation, our eyes vainly battling to remain alert in case that crack in the curtain should allow a momentary glimpse of Old St Nick.

In church on this particular Christmas Eve there was little of the solemnity normally attributed to religious occasion. People chatted openly, wishing each other the compliments of the season, while the Irish contingent was even more exuberant than usual with its Yuletide greetings. In the most reverent passages of the Mass one of them might snap out of a snooze and drunkenly bellow, 'God bless ye, Farder.' Snoring like circular saws, they unsettled even the hardiest priest. This was accepted and found relatively amusing seeing that even intoxicated with Guinness and whisky, it was impossible to keep a good Irishman out of church.

What was not acceptable was my brother's behaviour. Having attained an age where drinking was allowed in moderation, he had left earlier in the evening to indulge in a little light refreshment with his friends. My parents were liberal enough to turn a blind eye to the drinking laws, provided it was understood that he monitored his intake. I was still too young to indulge, so it was up to my brother to tread this new territory. However, when he arrived it seemed he might have trodden a little too far, for as he walked down the aisle to the vestry I detected an uncertainty in his stride. My father said nothing, but a momentary glance transmitted to my mother signalled trouble.

Performing as an altar boy at Midnight Mass was regarded as the *coup de grâce*, a night when many were called but few were chosen, and tonight the lucky few got to wear the good robes. Scarlet cassocks with pearl buttons and white linen tops rustled with starched efficiency in the procession to the altar. My brother had been chosen to lead the parade and hold aloft the incense chalice, an ornate dispenser held by an array of jangling gold pulleys and chains. There was little time for my brother's condition to subside, for no sooner had he disappeared into the vestry than the organ was pumped up and the pageant began. It was customary for the priests and altar boys to enter from the rear of the church and approach the altar up the centre aisle. As a spiritual rendition of 'Hark the Herald Angels Sing' began, I could see that my father was afraid to turn and witness my brother's approach. A sound idea on his part, for as I turned there was my elder brother weaving up the aisle, his cassock buttoned odd to even and swinging what was supposed to be swayed. Those closest to the aisle ducked in order to avoid his erratic oscillation of the holy sphere. To add to our embarrassment the hem of his cassock was caught in the cuff of his trousers, exposing a pair of blinding green Dayglo socks. Wearing a suppressed grin that enhanced his drunkenness, he turned to my parents and sang, 'Piss on urth an mershe mile ... ' The Irish, picking up on my brother's condition, made things worse by taking him to heart and egging him along with a series of ribald cheers. Once he reached the altar he seemed to mellow and, with the aid of the younger priests, he settled into the background where he sat and hummed merrily to himself for the remainder of the Mass.

On the home front I did nothing to cause my parents grief, even though at times I may have leapt before I looked when it came to pet projects and illicit ventures. One that comes to mind

69

and makes a strong point for adolescent stupidity was the time I took advantage of my mother's account at the village shop. In order to attract the attention of small boys, breakfast cereal manufacturers would place cheap toys in their boxes to sell more of their product. More often than not it would be a series, something collectible, something that had you coming back for more. It just so happened that Weetabix, my own particular favourite, was offering a detective set including magnifying glass, fingerprint kit and police badge. Once I started collecting something I became fanatical, and in order to procure these prizes I stooped to a system that was not so much daring as it was dumb. Having an account made it possible to pop into the village shop and charge up items without question, as my mother often sent me to pick up odds and ends for the house. Each time this happened I would add a box of Weetabix to the list until I found myself returning with alarming frequency. In fact, in the span of four hours one day I visited the store three times for more cereal. I'm unaware whether the shopkeeper was at all perplexed by the inordinate amount of Weetabix our family was consuming, as she merely handed over the goods and dutifully jotted down the purchase on my mother's account. Like a wild animal I dragged my booty to the far corner of the vegetable garden, ripping apart the box in order to check my prize. I was becoming increasingly annoyed to find I was duplicating the items I already had, but nowhere as annoyed as my father when confronted with the fact that, according to our grocery bill, our family had purchased fifteen boxes of Weetabix in one week. I was not a thinker, just a compulsive collector. Unfortunately my father met me head on with his compulsive brand of punishment. Silence.

I'm proud to say that my parents never struck me in anger although God knows they had cause. Whenever one of us did something to displease them it was always the silent treatment that we received and, believe me, there was nothing worse. When you're used to parental love, the way we were, alienation from that love in any form is crushing.

And each day, I learn just a little bit more . . .

There was an old blue transistor radio that my father carried while doing the farm work. It accompanied him from morning till night and then accompanied me to bed, for night was the time when it was possible to tune in to Radio Luxemburg. The reception was terrible, but for me the radio was the key to the best of all possible worlds. The BBC broadcast the occasional pop show, such as Brian Matthews's 'Saturday Club' and Alan Freeman's 'Pick of the Pops', but with Radio Luxemburg there was a hint of rebellion in the airwaves. It exuded a sense of disorganization, making you feel you were challenging the big guns by tuning in, and through this station I kept abreast of the 'beat boom', as it was quaintly christened by the media. I learned that the Beatles had conquered America and had released their first feature film called *A Hard Day's Night*. There was also an abundance of new bands: Gerry and the Pacemakers, Billy J. Kramer and the Dakotas, and the Searchers, to name a few, all of them notching up their own string of hits. The sexual innuendo of the Stones' 'It's All Over Now' sounded wicked and wild spluttering out of the tiny speaker, as in those days rock and roll really was made for the radio. It came through raw and edgy, full of intense excitement and restless aggression with no frills attached to extract the vitality of the natural rhythm. There was none of today's plastic surgery to nip and tuck the mistakes, just desperate energy burning through the static and branding itself in my heart.

. . . I don't know why but I do know what for.

The subject of rebels was never more appropriate than in the case of gypsies. From early spring and well into the summer they came to Highgate Lane and I would see them from the bus on my way to school. Unwelcome to the villagers, they were regarded as shiftless and lazy. The womenfolk would come into the village and go from door to door selling clothes-pegs and heather, while the menfolk dealt mainly in scrap. However, the original Romanies who came to graze their horses and park their wagons on the roadside were the genuine article, and I remember how we would scurry along the hedgerows at a safe distance to observe their lifestyle. Their large wooden wagons on great spoked wheels were painted vivid colours and decorated with jangling brass lanterns. Heavily embroidered curtains hung over the front and back, behind which they slept when the weather drove them in from under the stars. Swarthy, brooding and colourful, they were free spirits, relying on their wits to survive, keeping to themselves and running their affairs by a code of honour. With time their authenticity began to fade, the colour washing out with the seasons as the caravans turned to chrome and metal. Small dingy trailers towed by rusting Fords and Vauxhalls replaced proud horses in gleaming harnesses. The true gypsies vanished and it was hard to believe the pinched-faced men with darting eyes who took their place could be the same breed. Gypsies, tinkers, call them what you will, they were not what they had once been; the new breed was a blot on the original, giving credence to the manner in which they were thought of and treated. As the land changes, so do those who live upon it, but I know the true gypsy still exists in the spirit in which he was forged, trapped as the modern world closes in.

. . . you have to clean the oyster to find the pearl.

By the summer of '64 I learned that my school was introducing an additional year which would be voluntary for those who wished to advance their education. This is certainly not the reason I re-enlisted – it was just another twelve months to avoid the inevitable nine to five. The fourth year having been reasonably comfortable, I imagined the fifth should be a doddle. The Old House had by now become nothing more than a think-tank, a retreat where amidst the remnants of my past projects I sat and plotted the course of my dubious future. I didn't feel odd wallowing in the simple pleasure of acting out my fantasies, but I was beginning to feel the sting of change coursing through my veins. All the things which in the last few months had been coming to a boil in my consciousness were now begging to be given expression. At school my friendship with Danny remained firm and the pleasure we received in each other's company was adequate, while in the village most of my peers had run the gauntlet of my whacky schemes. I desired a stronger bond of friendship, for if I was to embark on the true adventure of teenage rebellion, I needed the tools with which to apply myself to the cause. What I needed was a gang!

Six

My introduction to Eddie, Rick and Steve came with advance warning from heaven, for it was from a great height that I first became acquainted with the three individuals with whom I shared the most important years of my teenage life. It was a warm Sunday afternoon in the autumn of '64 and in a moment of unbridled compassion my eldest brother had invited me to join him and his friends for a bike ride to the nearby village of Spridillby. At this time I had no form of transportation to call my own and it was only after much cajolement that I managed to borrow a bike from one of my brother's far from benevolent pals.

Bikes were without a doubt the teenage transport of the day and it was a luxury indeed to be the possessor of anything mobile equipped with an engine. Motorcycles were a grand acquisition of the hard worker on double overtime or the diligent greaser with a miserly grip on his dole cheque. Cars were the stars, the jewel in the crown, the unobtainable, and oh-so-cherished by those lucky enough to own the lowliest of heaps. The youth with a car was both popular and revered, the world was his oyster and the country roads his Indie 500.

The day was quiet and the road was free of mobile hierarchy as we rode along, the only sound the whirring of our chains as we free-wheeled into the dips and curves of the narrow lane. The heat waves before us held stationary in the air powdered yellow clouds of pollen, which burst on our nut-brown chests as we cycled through them. There were the customary smells of dried grass and new-mown hay as the warm amber of the sun beat down on us. Old stone cottages dotted the roadside, basking in tranquillity behind the coarse foliage of so many floral walls. As

73

we cycled past, the occasional farm dog leapt unexpectedly into view, pursuing our rear wheels with playful aggression. Laughing nervously, our hearts racing, we chastized these four-legged foot pads as our own feet spurred our bikes beyond the jaws of provocation.

The tiny village of Spridillby lay before us, secluded in a small incline and shadowed from detection by a dense layer of giant chestnut trees. The moment we zipped into the cavernous opening of foliage, the light was gone and we were enveloped by a counterfeit twilight and stung by a radical change in temperature. The coolness of this protected stretch was greatly appreciated, and we came to a halt to catch our breath and let the soothing breeze dry our sticky skin. The sun was completely blocked from the sky, the chestnuts trapping us in this fabulous vacuum as the wind rustled among the leaves performing a hushed lullaby.

The vast entrance through which we had ridden shed the only light. Like a giant mouth forming an unpronounceable 'O', it swallowed and digested us in the magic within. Dwarfed by the enormity of it all, I stood astride my crossbar and stared open-mouthed into the density of the lush roof overhead. It was at that moment that the conker hit my two front teeth, narrowly missing the gaping orifice an inch below. My teeth shuddered and my mouth snapped shut in protest. The pain was minimal but the joke was on me, and my friends sniggered offensively. As I was thinking to myself *of all the conkers in all the trees* . . . another one beaned me on the back of the head. By now my brother and his pals, who were rapidly becoming my least favourite people, had crumpled into a hysterical heap in the middle of the road. Suddenly, without warning, a hailstorm of conkers poured from the trees with wanton fury, smooth round missiles zeroing in with deadly accuracy. The laughter ceased and panic became the order of the day as we stumbled around disconnecting from each other and making a beeline for our bikes. Heading out with a volley of conkers whistling around my ears, I happened to glance back into the trees long enough to see the triumphant gleam of three unfamiliar faces.

Routed from Spridillby, we rode home in stony silence. I inquired into the identity of our assailants and after much grumbling and muttered threats of revenge managed to extract their names. Aside from being referred to as 'bloody Sprid yobos', I was told I could thank Eddie Page and Rick East and his brother Steve for the rising welts on my body. However, it was not revenge that reigned supreme in my mind on our slow ride home. As I pondered our ambush, the trace of a smile crossed my lips. I didn't know these guys but, for some strange reason, I already liked them.

Around the same time as the Spridillby incident a youth club was opened down the road in Doramby. Youth clubs were becoming increasingly popular in our region and we reacted to them as a godsend. They were founded on the notion that in the outlying villages surrounding the main towns there was nothing to entertain the restless teens. If you were over eighteen you had the pubs, but beneath that blessed of all ages there was little more than a dark street corner on which to stage your entertainment. Youth clubs gathered the strays and threw them together in one place a couple of nights a week. They were generally little more than a village hall with a ping-pong table and a record player and, in Doramby's own particular club, no more than a dozen teenagers could be found standing around sipping warm Cokes on a Friday night. The laws were lax and there was little that could be deemed a 'no no'. The older boys occasionally smuggled in bottles of brown ale, but even this eluded the attention of the overseer of the proceedings, usually an unenthusiastic volunteer from the church committee who sat nodding off over a paperback in his lap. I had heard tell that there were youth clubs north of Market Slaten boasting attendances of twenty-five to thirty people, inviting members from far and wide. To me this was living: all the new faces, new music and adventure that lay so near but yet so far away. Alas, for a lad with little kindred spirit for his contemporaries in the village and no bike to call his own, what hope was there of travelling farther afield than his own back yard?

My redemption from this fate came to the club one night in the form of the three boys whom I had last seen leering at me from a chestnut tree. What may have been a ground-rule for the democratic clubs to the north was not necessarily a practice held by the members of Doramby's own cultural mecca. Outsiders, although not lynched on sight, were treated with the utmost caution and shown little courtesy. Guests were normally friends of existing members, but the welcome mat was unceremoniously removed in the advent of the unwanted, and when Eddie, Rick and Steve walked in the front door I expected a show-down. If good and evil were ordained to clash that night, the confrontation was cancelled due to lack of interest. Beside a few cold stares and some awkward gawking, nothing happened. The show-down fizzled out and my brother, being his personable self, made the first move towards a treaty. By the end of the evening they were all happily puffing on the peace-pipe with the utmost intentions of goodwill.

In the course of the next few weeks the three newcomers became little more than nodding acquaintances. My brother nurtured their friendship with vigour, but I detected a twinkle in their eyes that did not quite mesh with my brother's values on the straight and narrow. He was studious, courteous and athletic, three attributes I felt he would be hard-pressed to find in Eddie and the Easts. On juvenile intuition alone, it was not hard to see that they wore the finer points in life like a millstone around their necks. Rick seemed the most intense and, if there was an academic mind amongst them, I imagined it must be his. It was Rick who seemed more drawn to my brother than the others and it was on this fact that I drew my conclusions. He was of average height with traces of baby fat still visible in his remarkably fresh face. Stocky and fleshy without the excess being too apparent, he wore his strikingly blond hair in a greaseless pompadour.

My introduction to them was inevitable, and it was Rick's elder brother Steve who was to cement our friendship with the common bond of words and music. Steve was the tallest of the three with a rougher-hewn complexion and long kinky hair. His appearance was intimidating and his look could easily have been translated as aggressive. In actuality he was the most docile of the bunch with an impassive broody nature, and it was to this that I was attracted. Steve appeared lost in himself much of the time and, seeing a similarity in this aspect of his character, I felt compelled to make the first move towards a stronger friendship. After this initial effort we all three fell together like the lost pieces of an incomplete puzzle, inching into our allotted slots as naturally as our names were to become synonymous with each other. Seeing that the ball was out of his court, my brother relinquished any ties he might have made with the boys and reverted to the rigours of spartan competition.

Rick and Steve were the sons of decidedly working-class parents, but Eddie was an entirely different kettle of kippers. His father was Spridillby's premier landowner, a man whose daily duties included surveying his property from the front seat of an expensive car. Eddie himself was a mockery of everything you might have expected him to be. The possessor of an extraordinarily dry sense of humour, he took life in his stride and his down-to-earth honesty reflected itself in his chiselled features. Swarthy and bright-eyed, he was the archetypal farm boy, fit and strong. Together the four of us made an uncompromising quartet, and with summer's end and the coming of a new school term, we were beginning to meld into each other's lives with natural ease. The adventure was beginning and though each of us possessed different attributes, it was not hard to fathom that we had come together for the common cause of discovery and fun.

With my fifth year of school came an unexpected bonus: not only were we the guinea pigs of a new system but I was informed I was to become a prefect. I was excited by this, but refrained from digging too deep into the reasons behind my promotion. I had a sneaking suspicion there had been a limited response to the optional year and a lack of legitimate candidates for the job. With the attitude 'something is better than nothing', I had been decorated. The bestowing of this title was not a subject I dwelled upon, but along with the superiority factor the fifth year guaranteed, it seemed to me that '65 promised to be a relatively easy ride.

By the end of '64 things were taking shape nicely. With my newly acquired fascist station at school and my new-found friends in the home camp, I was also taking steps to improve my capabilities in life's romantic sweepstakes. Those girls remaining in the fifth year were not at all bad, as what was left after the weeding-out years was the *crème de la crème*. They were attractive and tidy, if not a little self-centred, but then I was all for a modicum of vanity, and at least their brains were bolted down and didn't slide out their ears when they took a right-hand turn. Several of the girls were from Bealby and Hempton, two villages boasting youth clubs that smacked of pizazz. They pointed out that there was an open invitation to attend any time I wished and, taking into consideration the fact that I was attracted to a well-built beauty from Hempton, the offer washed over me in waves of wanderlust.

Daphne, the girl in question, aside from obvious exterior qualities, was a shy compassionate girl who, although initially cautious to advances, was to become my first true experience. The Mickey Mouse days were over and I was instilled with a new confidence, although not yet ready to perch atop a podium to assert my masculinity, preferring to take on the guise of reckless romantic; a sort of Cyrano de Bergerac without the nose.

Along with the perks of seniority came a choice of classes and authority to roam the streets during lunch hour. Danny and I abused both these privileges, opting for a system in which our choice of classes so confused the teachers that none of them was quite sure where we were supposed to be and when. The former was often the Waterloo Café, an establishment that was to become one of several locations deemed as headquarters and major pit-stops in the years to come. Situated in a narrow road off the main street, the Waterloo was packed on weekends, but on weekdays was relatively empty except for a regular lunch crowd. It was nothing to look at, a hole in the wall actually, small and indistinguished but somehow cosy and inviting. There was a juke-box, several pinball machines and the erratic service of Herman and Magda, two German immigrants who ran the place with good-natured efficiency. Magda tended to become nervous at times, a reaction brought on by Herman's bullish manner and the clientele's lack of etiquette, but all the same I enjoyed the place immensely. I had yet to spend legitimate hours there, but the stolen moments we made available to ourselves were fun. While our fellow-classmates were consumed by noxious gases in the science lab, we consumed ham rolls and beans on toast amid the deep-fried splendour of the Waterloo.

My horizons were expanding with the ever-deepening friendship developing between the boys and me, and by January of the new year we had become inseparable. Whether in a pack or in pairs, we were four aces destined to be a good hand in any game. Our bicycles began to take us everywhere; they were the most important piece of equipment we possessed. By this time I had acquired a reliable hand-me down of my own, as without one you were stranded and isolated like a knight without a steed or a cowboy without a gun. They were a necessity, a machete of sorts with which to explore the teenage jungle, for now it was possible to venture farther afield and those youth clubs we had heard so much about were finally within our grasp.

Each evening of the school week we kept in contact by phone. While Eddie and I shared the luxury of a phone in the home, Rick and Steve were forced to use the public call box. Rick was a technician of sorts and skirted the twopenny charge by skilfully tapping the digits with his finger, thus breaking the law and saving his change. We all attended school in separate locations. I was at Market Slaten, Rick and Steve were in Lincoln and Eddie spent the weeks away at boarding school in Grimsby, returning on Friday nights in time to be filled in on the weekend agenda.

Back then the phone was not the abused device it has become today. In many village households such as ours it was a respected piece of equipment not to be taken for granted. My father kept a watch on all outgoing calls and anyone on the phone for over five minutes would be the recipient of much parental 'harumphing'. His theory was that it was a device designed to transmit business details and not a toy on which to prattle for hours. When it did ring it was normally to convey the clipped conversation of farmers calling to confirm appointments with my father.

'Ev'nin' Mester. Breslaw here from up Swarby way. When yer cumin' round to see me beast?'

'Friday suit you, say nine-thirty?'

'Aye, Friday grand. Ta. 'Bye.'

Besides these we received few other calls, until dull uneventful evenings in Spridillby drove the Easts to the call box. We chatted most nights at great length, my father harumphing till he was blue in the face while we discussed our 'best laid schemes o' mice an' men'.

Making friends for the world to see . . .

———————————

Bealby was twelve miles from Bramby on the other side of Market Slaten. A picturesque village under the steep slope of the Wolds, it was regarded as one of the prettiest in Lincolnshire. It had been the home of Alfred Lord Tennyson and in the village hall on the edge of his estate we came to visit Bealby's renowned youth club. There was no doubt it had the edge on Doramby's sad excuse, and although it was far from being 'Rick's Café American', it did exude a warm and friendly atmosphere. The music was loud and the crowd was a mixture of acquaintances from school, local folk and the odd stranger. Being newcomers, we attracted a certain amount of attention and as the conversation buzzed between the scattered groups, we sensed appreciation in the eyes of the females present. Fresh faces were few and far between, and it struck us that in evolving our free-wheeling spirit the possibilities of popularity in this region were limitless. If we could nurture this image of good-natured camaraderie combined with a reckless sense of nomadic pride then it might be possible to carve ourselves quite a reputation, not to mention our effect upon the feminine faction who would be magnetically drawn to our gypsy will. A lot of this had to do with the way I saw our group in my own mind, and once again the need to be different became the number one priority. In order to achieve this it was necessary to mould our image into something more than the average gang. It was here that we began to evolve into what was once described as *'a walking contradiction partly truth and partly fiction'*. Instead of bending to one trend we borrowed from many, compiling our own particular style. Incorporating a hint of arrogance in our overall make-up, we managed to establish a territorial supremacy within a very short time. I can say with pride that this was accomplished without a hint of violence and with a great deal of bullshit.

In order to embellish our stature, we became masterful in the art of public relations. We merely fed fabricated stories of our luck in love and battle into the jungle telegraph and within a week they had spread throughout the watering holes of the teenage populace. Although we impressed the majority, our claims were met with more than a little disbelief and distaste from the other male cliques. Their antagonism was marginal and we merely steered clear of any confrontation that might result in bloodlet-ting. But just in case, we used Steve's awesome presence as a front and concocted for him a killer image to keep us out of danger. Our ingenuity was astounding, and it was interesting to witness how individually we had become saddled with different images in the eyes of those around us. Steve was our defence, Rick became the baby-faced Don Juan and Eddie the devil-may-care character. I was our very own Baron Munchausen, laying the plans and plotting our lies, the silent instigator and overall *enfant terrible.*

Our reputation fully intact, we continued our conquest of the provinces. Along with Bealby we vanquished Hempton, where my voluptuous Daphne became the sudden aggressor and allowed me to fondle her breasts in the bicycle shed. Things were on the roll and I was beginning to reap the benefits of my own PR. If these supple beauties cupped in my hands represented the ignition, then I was fully prepared to find the key and fire up the engine. Alas, common decency denied me the right and it was made clear to me that the only approachable parts of her anatomy were from the naval up. So with our lips locked in passionate embrace and my hand trapped between her bra and breast, I decided that for now there was no price on time; after all, we had only just begun to fight.

It was the dawn of the Mods and the inevitable clash between the old and new was not to be weighed out evenly in our area. The rural backwoods were Rocker strongholds and the train of fashion moved at a snail's pace between London and Lincolnshire. Although the likes of the Who were trailblazing a new trend in the cellars of suburban London, there was little to indicate that any of their fire was spreading to the provinces and the only feedback they seemed to be generating was from their own guitars. In and around Market Slaten, the dyed-in-the-wool Rocker still clung to his Buddy Holly records and danced to Bill Haley on a Saturday night. Serenading his bird with a constant stream of oldies on the juke-box, he became trapped in a time warp, clinging with nostalgic pride to the safety of that which he knew best. So while London began to swing, Lincoln and much of the north preferred to remain entrenched in the Fifties, living with a legacy of dead heroes. It was an ill wind that blew change this way. *'Keep a knockin' but you can't come in . . . '*

The boys and I with our high ideals wished to remain independent of any cause, preferring to become the radical fringe which paid allegiance to no one. We genuinely loved both the raucous rebellion of the old school and the hungry attack of the new breed but refused to be categorized in any way. Shunning

81

the uniform of any sect, we chose to establish our own non-committal look. There was no patent on our fashion and it was necessary to let ourselves be informed by whatever sources of the media helped us best.

I was still wetting my appetite on the likes of *Fab, Rave* and the rest, buying these magazines by the dozen and keeping up my fanatical following of the pop culture. Aside from the fanzines there was 'Ready Steady Go (Your Weekend Starts Here)', television's revolutionary rock show, which truly reflected the spirit of the music scene. It transmitted information on clothes, dance, even gestures and slang to the whole British teenage Isles. The programme embodied the early Sixties all the way down to Cathy McGowan, its daffy but affable hostess, whose giggly fan-like presence made it all the more irresistible. It was totally unconventional and ultimately the bands performed live due to the Musicians' Union ruling on miming. Once this happened the show became one of chaotic magic, and with no restrictions the bands became totally engrossed in what they were playing, going way over schedule. It was a one-of-a-kind kaleidoscopic pro-gramme through which we starved fanatics on the border-line got to view the best of British rock, along with shows featur-ing legendary American performers rarely seen in Britain. People such as James Brown and Otis Redding came into our living rooms on a Friday night and left us ragged and panting to begin the weekend. God how I loved it, every single sweat-filled second! If rock was a river, then I wished to drown in it. There was no way I could pledge allegiance to any one faction, whether it was Little Richard or the Rolling Stones, Buddy Holly or the Beatles; it was all for one. The Who, the Animals, Elvis or Eddie Cochran, each invigorated me in a different way. If you put them all in a blender and poured the mixture out, you ended up with the same thing – a steaming bowl of rock and roll!

The four of us shared this view and voiced our opinions openly. Then in March of '65 something happened that cemented our style completely and wrote the code for the hobo days to come. While tuning in to my beloved Luxemburg one night, I chanced upon a sound totally foreign to me. Cutting through the thunder of guitars and drums came the strident chording of a lone acoustic accompanied by a wailing harmonica. A voice that raised the flesh on the nape of my neck spat out an amazing array of words in a plaintive nasal whine, leaving me speechless. Never had I encountered anything like it. I'd heard folk music before, but nothing like this. This wasn't your 'Here we go round the maypole' stuff, it wasn't even one of those nice folksy ditties I used to hear Burl Ives sing. This was a voice like broken glass, full of anguish and cynicism, tearing at the establishment and warning that *'Your sons and your daughters are beyond your command for the times they are a changin'.'*

The initial effect of Bob Dylan's music, and this song in particular, left me in a state of euphoria, followed by a frantic scramble to spread the word. This was something Steve had to hear! We regarded ourselves as the musical connoisseurs of the group, the ones most likely to break into an entire repertoire of material at any given opportunity. But this, this was something really to sink your teeth into. These words conveyed more than just 'I love you' and 'My baby left me'; they spoke of restlessness and discontent, conjuring up a wealth of images that tugged at my spirit and put the highway in my eyes. I tended to get more than a little carried away by events such as these, but looking back it was a healthy shot of natural exuberance, and the pleasure I derived from being the first to make such a discovery was genuine.

In the weeks and months that followed this awakening, Bob Dylan and his imitators became the mentors of our movement. I scrimped and saved every penny in order to attain the backlog of Dylan albums. I recall turning up at Doramby Youth Club one night with a copy of 'Highway 61 Revisited'. I had every intention of converting the underprivileged, but after several bars of 'From a Buick 6' someone unceremoniously dragged the needle off the record and replaced it with 'Beatles for Sale'. Undaunted by this effort to cast pearls before swine, I was content in the knowledge that I was able to convince my cohorts that the message in the music was one for us. Steve was equally as infatuated by these ideals, and it was not hard to swing Rick and Eddie over to our way of thinking. Very soon the four of us acquired a definite uniform. Inspired by the new-wave folk hero and his common bond with the working man, we dressed in denim and ditched our bikes in favour of the riding thumb. If we were to mould ourselves into a counterpart of the idealistic American hobo, it was important to rely on our own resourcefulness in order to get from here to there; after all, Woody Guthrie never rode a bike.

. . . the highway looks like it never did,
Lord, it looks so sweet and so free . . .

If my mother ever regretted that her cooking was an inspiration, she never showed any sign of it. Her talent for making the simplest fare fit for a king became a mess-hall bugle continuously summoning my friends to table throughout my teenage years. Brilliant in their subtlety, they arrived regular as clockwork the moment the mitted glove removed something from the oven. Always full of stock apologies and polished excuses, their sudden appearance was put down to bad timing and inconsideration. Of course it was all a charade and no one ever believed otherwise, as they were never turned away and always made welcome. My brother may have grunted disapproval as he took inventory of his chips, but on the whole it was just another place-setting for our growing family. This situation only goes to demonstrate the way in which we shared our lives. Whether it was a nourishing meal or the loan of your best Argyll socks, it showed dependency on your friends, the commitment to come through at all times.

We invariably stayed at each other's houses and while our home was known for its liberal canteen, Eddie's was considered the Spridillby Hilton and thus the capitalist centre of our dwellings. There was simply more room at Eddie's; Rick and Steve's was fine, but when all was said and done it was council-house cramped. After a long hike home, several teenage boys with smelly feet tossing and turning in a single bed is rock bottom on the scale of comfort. Any chance to stay at the Page spread was basically fab, although whether in reality it was any more comfortable is debatable. It was obviously the enormity and grandeur that appealed to us, along with the fact that we could get fresh cream on tap, thanks to Mr Page's fine dairy herd. Eddie would pour gallons of it on his Shredded Wheat, a cereal he was particularly fond of and consumed by the boxful. I never questioned his addiction, merely watching in dumb amazement, impressed by such gluttony. This may seem like a pretty insignificant memory but it was bloody amazing if you were there at the time.

Our parents were a truly varied bunch but not untypical of the often denied but unequivocal British class system. Where that placed my family in the grand illusion I'm not too sure, but I would hazard a guess and stick a pin in the arse of the middle class. I respected my parents totally, and while I often disagreed with my father's authority and more often than not disobeyed it, there was always at the back of my mind gratification for his logic. This, coupled with my mother's shy wisdom, made for smooth sailing most of the time. In retrospect, the East household was in a state of continuous civil war and deciphering who ruled was a game played at a safe distance. Any laws laid down by Rick and Steve's long-suffering parents were unceremoniously hurled back in their faces. Rick's constant references to his father as 'yer gimp', due to his obvious limp, left visitors noticeably uncomfortable. Suffice to say that in this working-class home the spirit of Wat Tyler lived on in Rick and Steve. It was easy for me to be ignorant and unconcerned by their feuds back then, but what haunts me now is the way this open hostility by her children laid waste to Mrs East. The uncertainty of her husband's wage packet and the constant bickering had turned her into a nervous, highly-strung shadow of her former self. She seemed constantly in pain, for ever reeling from verbal abuse. Unfortunately things never changed and time never seemed to heal the cuts that went with her to the grave.

Eddie, on the other hand, lived in a world of open-ended rules and I sometimes wondered whether his parents even knew he was there. They were not uncaring; on the contrary, Mrs Page was a charming woman always bustling through the house content in the arms of domesticity, while Eddie's dad Stan was a tailor-made Tatler parody with true society leanings. He would cruise the countryside's better public houses in search of idle chatter on horse and hound, happy as the Lord of the Manor. There was a great deal of space in the family, of which Eddie continually made use, ducking in and out without the hammer of parental control nailing him to any set rules.

We gathered wherever it was conducive to at the time. At my house we ate and watched hours of 'Untouchables' re-runs; at the

Easts' we tinkered with our bikes, and at Eddie's we ponced around the grounds with delusions of grandeur. In this setting we knew full well it was just a game, aware in our hearts that you can't make a silk purse out of a sow's ear.

Once a year Bartley's Fun Fair came to Market Slaten. Passing the town square on our way to school, we could see the trucks unloading the wooden frames and canvas that made up the rides and sideshows. Without this annual treat, few of us were privy to the pleasure of a carnival atmosphere, as the closest permanent sights of this nature were the coastal resorts of Skegness and Cleethorpes. Bartley's was no extravaganza; the town square was unable to accommodate much more than a central structure housing the dodgems and a dozen or so smaller attractions. All this was packed into an area of approximately 500 square feet, so you can imagine that the scale of entertainment was limited. Nevertheless the prospect of an evening's entertainment was thrilling and I curbed my joy and counted the seconds until I returned home to inform the troops to prepare for all the fun of the fair.

After appealing to my father's good nature, he consented to give us a lift into town providing we didn't drag him out of bed later to retrieve us. In the past I had forced my pyjama-clad parent out of his warm bed to pick up his stranded son in any amount of strange places. He never did let me down, but the disgusted expression on his face when he turned up was enough to make me wish I'd walked. Walking was something we were used to by now, but if the hour was ungodly or the weather too fierce, I was forced to flee to the phone box and dial the distress signal. That night as we piled into the car the last thing on our minds was how we were going to get home, and I imagine my thoughts were on my impending date with Daphne. I had arranged for her to bring along several of her friends, hoping this rendezvous might cause sparks to fly between my pals and hers.

Our turnout was noteworthy that evening. By now we were all proud possessors of Beatle boots, after waiting an eternity for them to arrive at 'Banger' Halls, Market Slaten's very own boutique, a cross between Mary Quant and Marks & Spencer. Being the only store carrying anything remotely fashionable, it was here that we purchased most of our attire. Lincoln's shops were inaccessible on a regular basis, so Banger became our tailor.

Looking like an emaciated Hank Marvin, he was a high-powered salesman who in a pinch could have sold a fish supper to a dead cat. Moving around the shop like a deranged stick-insect he would tear down cartons from the shelves and empty them on to the floor in front of us. 'Just fab, boys . . . the very latest . . . super quality stuff . . . ' We doubted this but were dutifully impressed by his attentiveness.

We were certainly not designer detailed by the spring collections but our erratic sense of dress is cause for amusement on reflection. It was not unusual to see us in Beatle boots and ice-blue jeans with a denim jacket over a Dave Clarke shirt. Mixed thinking makes mad hatters, and while Banger was no doubt laughing all the way to the bank, we were perfectly happy sitting in the back of my dad's car looking like a combination of Gene Vincent, Jack Kerouac and Dr Kildare.

We were dropped off across the street from the town square and after a renewed assurance that there would be no late-night phone calls, my father returned into the night leaving trouble to fend for itself. The distinct sounds and smells of the fair assaulted our senses the minute we strode amongst the gaily painted tents and stalls. This was merely a section of a larger fair which divided up in the early spring to accommodate the smaller towns before reassembling in expansive pastures for the summer season. We were grateful for just a slice of the pie and, with our fags dangling from our lips with strategic cool, we headed for the dodgems, the core of the fair. Hanging around the railings surrounding them were groups of boys and girls jockeying for position in the eagle's nest. From here it was possible to survey the surroundings while retaining adequate accessibility to the roving bands of loose women. The smell of candy floss and onions hung in the air like a sticky cloud as the rattling poles behind the bumper cars trailed sparks of electricity across the wire roof. The music was loud and dated and echoed through the square, richocheting off the surrounding buildings with little finesse. The overall quality was tinny but gave off a pleasant hurdy-gurdy effect that applied itself perfectly to the atmosphere. The fair was that kind of place, one of visual magic aided and abetted by a roller-coaster of sounds designed to drum away the drudgery of the working day.

We located the girls and inched in beside them, making sure any body contact would be gratifying to both parties. It was always interesting to see the girls from school in their civvies and tonight was no exception. Daph, who had a habit of always looking unnaturally lustful for her age, had brought along the Meddle twins and Priscilla Bradford. All three were classmates of mine and very pretty. Jackie and Joan, the twins, were indistinguishable, a fact I found unsettling as anyone dating them could become extremely confused and wind up in the most embarrassing situations. A secret confided to one could mistakenly be related to the other, making it possible for them to maintain a stranglehold on their suitors. However, this didn't seem to deter my friends, who regarded them as one and the same body, their intentions having little depth.

Priscilla Bradford on the other hand, although pleasant, came across as a little holier than thou, an attitude that registered with my friends as 'look, but don't touch'. I felt Priscilla never got over the fact that she didn't make it to grammar school, and thought it in her best interest to conduct herself with dignity and diplomacy. How she got this impression of grammar school girls was beyond me! Most of the ones I knew were no different from their secondary school counterparts; they just played hockey by the rules and wore uniforms. So as Eddie, Rick and Steve quibbled over the twins, Daph and I climbed into a vacant dodgem and proceeded to thump our way through the pack, avoiding contact with any delinquent types.

The fair attracted some unsavoury characters including the biker gangs from Farshem, notorious for their dislike of anything remotely human. It was these thugs, who wore their studded leathers like a second skin and parted crowds like the Red Sea, whom we of the oh-so-cool steered clear of lest we fracture our standing in the community. As Daph and I careered happily in circles, I noticed that many of the girls lounging on the rails were flashing coy smiles at the men working the ride. Momentarily I was flushed with jealousy at these true independent rebels of the road and, try as I might, it was hard for me to shake off my envy.

There was something about working for the fair and hanging on the back of the rides with bravado that appealed to the girls. The image we were desperate to project was living proof in these carnival cowboys, and it was depressing to think we were merely toys in the light of the real thing. Jumping from one car to another they collected the money and made a string of dates that could be kept, concluded and left behind in the trail of the first truck out at sunrise. As the night progressed we tried our luck on the various stalls. We hurled darts, burst balloons, fired rifles and sank bean bags, obtaining a selection of cheap novelties and stuffed animals. Our winnings were immediately shoved into the arms of our trailing females. Heaven forbid that the Robin Hoods of rural Lincs be seen clutching pink nylon poodles and plastic bags of goldfish!

The Temple Arms loomed behind us like a dry throat, its rustic leaded windows shedding a welcoming light for the thirsty traveller as we sat outside on the stoop like a bunch of farm dogs tethered by our age. The girls were uninterested in our inaccessibility to this watering hole, and while Priscilla consulted her bus timetable, the twins began to whine about hamburgers and toffee apples. Things were getting crabby and I detected Daph's companions were cramping the boys' style. Eddie, being a lad of little diplomacy, had taken his leave earlier, obviously disgusted by Priscilla's refusal to renege on her virtue. Feeling under pressure, I urged Daph to accompany me on a walk and leave the lowing herd to debate their next move. I had no doubt Rick and Steve could fend for themselves and would soon detach from the pack and hook up with Eddie back on the front line. With the sound of the fair fading behind us, we walked hand in hand through the alleyway leading to the churchyard. Daph's heels made a resounding click on the cobblestones, giving advance warning to the snoggers of approaching detection. The churchyard was notorious and on a night like this a hive of couples could be found in all sorts of compromising positions. The entire area was lit by two dim lamps giving the maximum light necessary to unfasten a bra clasp. The local Christians found this place a hotbed of sacrilegious sex maniacs intent on fornicating on hallowed ground. Indeed, there were signs that such acts had taken place, and try as I might it was hard to avert Daph's eyes from the used condoms hanging in the trees like strange translucent vegetation.

It was a paradox that while I was happy to find a quiet doorway in which to kiss and fondle Daphne's wealth of charms, I was equally restless to get back to my mates. I was not one who liked to miss out on anything and, in chauvinistic terms, I lived for the pack and lusted for the lamb. Once I had rushed through the motions for the benefit of my own desires and those of my amorous partner, I announced that in order to guarantee her safety it would be proper for me to escort her to the bus stop. This proved to be a wise move, for on arrival we learned that a panicked Priscilla was on the verge of organizing a search party. This could have proved quite amusing, as I pictured Priscilla tapping the shoulders of the hulking shadows in the graveyard inquiring of our whereabouts. Had she attempted this I doubt she would have returned; her bed for the night might well have been her bed for eternity. With Daph and her friends deposited safely into the care of Lincoln County Transport, I returned to look for the boys.

I found them under cover in the auctioning area perched on a stack of trestles, and by the look on their faces I could see their scouting trip had proved fruitless. The hour was late and most of the available girls had been snapped up. Soon the pubs would be turning out and for a short time before the fair closed down we could expect a rowdier crowd. Already the area around the dodgems had been commandeered by an older group waving beer bottles and screaming abuse at each other across the noisy circle. I could tell the boys felt cheated, but unfortunately there was little we could do about it now, as the last bus had left and with it most of our hopes. It was not the hour for tender young things, and concerned fathers had recalled their daughters to the fold. What we were left with was a mixture of young marrieds and blowzy factory girls who much preferred the company of Teds to tots. The whole scene was rather depressing and what had started out as a promising evening had fizzled out, leaving us a little out of our depth. It was one thing to be hot-shots on a level with our peers, but what we needed was to infiltrate the older crowd and make some contacts that might elevate us to a new standing.

We sat there for the next hour saying little and watching the drunks weave unsteadily through the stalls on their way home. Soon the crowds dispersed and the lines of coloured lights strung across the attractions began to flicker off, as one by one the fair workers emerged to roll down the canopies and board up the rides. Looking tired, they shuffled around in a mechanical daze doing what they had done so many times before. The fair didn't look quite as appealing now. Stale buns and apple cores littered the ground and toffee-wrappers and paper napkins clung to the workers' shoes. Melted ice-cream trickled between the cobbles, a sticky river disappearing down the drain into awaiting darkness. Depleted balloons rolled sadly into the street and bounced off the bonnets of passing cars for one last flight into the night air. The music ground to a halt and Bobby Vee was silenced in mid-song. Nothing was left but the dying sound of the generators as they expired with a defiant groan. Suddenly everyone was gone and we were alone in the half-light of the shed, staring out at the silence. Nothing stirred except for the sound of the flapping canopies as they struggled to free themselves in the rising wind. With a sigh of resignation we moved out of the shed as the storm clouds rolled in and it began to rain. Hitching up my collar against the howling night I turned to the others and searched their faces. Without a word the decision was made.

'Hello, Dad, guess what?'

Seven

It was a Saturday and we had decided to visit the youth club on the RAF base at Woolworth. Danny had suggested that if we were ever in the area we might want to check it out. I couldn't for the life of me imagine just 'happening' to be in the vicinity, as the base was in a characterless setting where identical houses stood side by side with regimented specification. Every lawn and shrub was manicured and clipped to coincide with the one next door, giving an overall impression of surrealism. However, it was territory unchartered and thus warranted a look-see.

When we walked we liked to sing, and on this particular occasion it was Donovan's 'Catch the Wind' that filled the afternoon air. The base was roughly three miles from Spridillby if you took the shortcut along the old runway that ran parallel to the main road. The strip was abandoned and had not seen a plane since the war. What remained was a sealed perimeter across from the airstrip, housing what looked like a prison camp. Dotted with KEEP OUT signs depicting skull and crossbones, the message was clearly driven home. This compound employed most of the servicemen stationed at Woolworth and was considered a top-secret operation. Everyone had their own theory as to what went on behind the barbed-wire fence with its searchlights and patrol dogs, the most dramatic being that it was an underground storage centre for the A-bomb. If this was so, it was ironic to think that the destructive power lying within was surrounded by much of the beauty it could eventually destroy. At the time, though, we acknowledged without fear the enormity of what might lie directly below us and strolled beyond the perimeter with our continued song serenading the birds on the wire and the bloke in the tower.

The flat expanse of the airstrip and its surroundings enabled us to be picked out and warmed by the sun as we filled our lungs and harmonized. *'In the chilly hours and minutes of uncertainty I want to be . . . '* There were violet buds bursting through the cracks below our feet. *'In the warm hold of your lovin' mind . . . '* Maybe they were growing right above the bomb. *'To feel you all around and to take your hand . . . '* Next to a rusting water tank a tethered donkey grazed on dry grass and thistles. *'Along the sand . . . '* I wondered if the donkey was bothered about the bomb. *'Ah, but I may as well try and catch the wind.'*

The runway was rarely used by everyday traffic and had become a rebel raceway for everything from potato crates on pram wheels to go-karts. It was perfect for speeding and the four of us had often raced our bikes here – the small round patch on the crotch of Rick's jeans reminded us of the last time.

Weeks earlier Rick and I had been cruising along this stretch when we decided to indulge in a little acrobatic stunt. Riding next to each other, we interlocked our inside arms while lifting our two free arms to meet above our heads. Being so close, my left handbrake managed to slip into the exposed right end of Rick's handlebars. Our front wheels locked, sending us sailing arm in arm through the air into Steve and Eddie who were several yards ahead. Untangling ourselves from the wreckage, Rick discovered that the collision had caused Eddie's handbrake to tear through his jeans leaving him within a millimetre of castration; a fraction closer and Rick would have been singing today's song in a higher register.

We found Danny swinging on a set of monkey bars next to the bus shelter. After asking him if he'd like a banana, I introduced him to the boys. He refused the banana and settled for a fag. (We smoked like chimneys back then, and whether I enjoyed it or indulged purely for effect, I don't recall. I do remember that Rick and Steve were coupon crazy and kept great wads of them stuffed in biscuit tins under their beds.)

It looked like a big night at the bus shelter and among those hanging around were a well-built blonde and a diminutive brunette. Danny told us they were officers' daughters and offered to introduce us providing we minded our manners. We promptly saluted them and inquired if officers' daughters were required to wear their medals on their knickers. Danny blushed and the girls smiled. Their names were Gaye and Mandy and both seemed happy to make our acquaintance. One of the drawbacks of being officers' daughters was that everything they said sounded as if their cheeks were lined with Polyfilla. However, once this initial language barrier was broken things proceeded nicely. There were masses of 'super' and 'triffic' in the conversation, leading Rick to the conclusion that while they might talk funny, it was a known fact posh birds liked a bit of rough. Relying on this, the night promised to yield the fruits of our labour. Gaye inquired if we were going to attend the youth club and we replied, 'That would be super!' Promising to meet them later, we left to inform Danny's mother she had four extra for tea.

The man who ran the youth club took an instant dislike to us. We were most definitely a scurrilous bunch of dissidents incapable of conforming to the regimental code by which he obviously ran the establishment. From the moment we walked through the door on that first evening until our unceremonious departure some months later, he was for ever scheming to terminate our membership. After all these years his name escapes me, but I believe it was something befitting his Marine bearing, like 'Bull' or 'Tug'. To us his comic manner christened him Sgt Fury. You know the type, flat top and white T-shirt, with battleships and 'Mother' all over his forearms; a mobile meat pie with nothing but veg inside. A look of disdain curled his lips as he eyed 'Long Live Rock' and 'War Kills' stencilled on the back of our combat jackets. This was enough to whiten his knuckles and collapse his crew-cut. For us it was merely a form of expression; to him it spelled trouble.

It was a tame crowd that attended, not one to challenge the cocky look of bravado we assumed as we surveyed the premises. The building was a standard Nissen hut converted into a recreation hall and filled with the obligatory games that I was beginning to find a little repetitious. At the rear of the building there was a maze of corridors and ante-rooms, most of which were empty. Several had been transformed into changing rooms and showering facilities for the use of the soccer teams that played on the pitch to the side of the building. Away from the keen eyes of our budding Führer, these darkened passages were a far more comfortable playground in which to smoke and chat. Here we were removed from the annoying camaraderie and competitive spirit of which our camp commandant was so fond. I think he preferred it this way, as the only time we had consented to join in had been for a no-holds-barred game of caveman's football. This lasted only ten minutes, in which time we broke three light fixtures, six windows and the nose of the camp commander's son. For those unfamiliar with the rules of caveman's football, there are no rules and the objective is simple. Your team merely has to get the ball from one end of the room to the other by fair means or foul – a thoroughly enjoyable experience for the lurking savage that lies dormant in us all.

The first evening began on a sour note as soon as we walked through the door. An officious little brat with squeaky-clean features and an Alfalfa hairdo stuck a battered trilby under our noses and demanded sixpence apiece. Offended by such a demeaning form of begging, we assaulted his outstretched *chapeau* with a barrage of pocket lint and toffee-wrappers, stifling his reaction of disapproval by whispered threats of life without kneecaps. Unlike most of the other youth clubs we frequented, the members here varied from the very young to the ageing simpleton. One of the strangest was a skinny girl of thirteen called Susan Weston who hung around the shadows along the hallways, jumping out without warning to grab the testicles of any passing male. Ordinarily we wouldn't have minded, as under normal circumstances this might prove quite pleasant. In this case, however, the sheer golem-like quality of the girl over-shadowed our desire to be groped and we decided to give her a wide berth at all times. Perhaps we could coax Sgt Fury to walk her way, leaving him high and dry in the choir of the castrati.

We were met as planned by Gaye and Mandy, who thought club life was 'super dooper' and 'would we chaps care for a little ping-pong?' Ping-pong was not what we had in mind but, in order to appease, ping-pong it had to be. While Rick and Steve batted politely, Eddie and I explored the club's nether regions, remaining on guard lest we encounter the phantom ball-grabber. It was quiet beyond the din of the decaying sound system, and in the stillness of a darkened changing room Eddie and I hatched a plan that might prove to be amusing in weeks to come. Pulling out our sheath knives we began to cut a series of small circular holes in the plywood wall that separated the locker room from the shower stalls.

Our visits to Woolworth became more frequent, based mainly on Rick's continued interest in Mandy. This was not a relationship based on a common bond in cultural affairs but purely on a desire to discover each other horizontally. The only ones who found it hard to raise a smile when we arrived were Sgt Fury and Alfalfa, who by this time had eradicated us from existence. The hat at the door was promptly withdrawn whenever we were seen approaching. With Rick and Mandy it seemed as if the hour was at hand and the 'Will you still respect me in the morning?' had been requested. The look in Rick's eyes did not betray the lie on his lips as we watched them slip through the rear door into the silence of the shadowed shower stalls. Bingo! The placement was perfect. We gave them enough time to secure themselves in a passionate embrace and waited until they were oblivious to anything around them. Soon enough the sound of heavy breathing rose above the stall like piston steam. Moving in quietly, we squatted before the trim holes that Eddie and I had so deftly whittled in the wall. Instead of allowing us access to Rick's amorous endeavours, we found the smooching twosome were leaning against our vantage point restricting our view. These portholes of ecstasy had not been carved to be covered by heaving buttocks and rather than be outsmarted I motioned Eddie and Steve to clamber on to the sinks in front of the partition. From here it was possible to peer down on our comrade without detection.

Directly below us Rick and Mandy were entwined in a mass of undergarments, their hands tearing in all directions in a futile attempt to gain access to corsets and Y-fronts. This was by no means a stylish seduction and the smack of elastic and the whizz of zips forced us to stifle our giggles, as slowly but surely some order of disrobement began to occur. Just as Rick was about to make some real contact, the steely claw of Susan Weston clutched my crotch sending my terrified scream ringing along the hallway like a death rattle. Rick and Mandy looked up in shock just in time to see the three of us lose our balance. In a desperate attempt to break our fall, we grabbed the top of the plyboard partition, and as we fell back so did the entire structure, including several washbasins and an entire row of lockers. The next thing we knew water was pouring forth in great geysers, shooting into the skylight six feet above, short-circuiting the complete area. We scrambled from under the wreckage in total darkness, my first thought being that Susan Weston's hand should be amputated in the cause of public decency. Infinitely more important at this particular moment was the reassembling of Rick and a swift exit, as we could clearly hear the heavy footfall of Sgt Fury's size tens bearing down on us. This incident kept us from Woolworth for quite some time, and we decided to return only when the will of high command sent our loathsome antagonist elsewhere.

With Woolworth off limits we were left with Bealby and Hempton. Bealby Youth Club was growing in stature, as they were now holding dances on a regular basis and attendance was flourishing. With it came the inevitable element of competition, making it necessary to be on our guard, as we could not allow new arrivals to challenge our authority. It was futile to think it possible to repel all boarders by brute force: what we needed was to maintain a level of amnesty. If it was possible to befriend the competition and ingratiate ourselves with them, we might ultimately assume a buddy system that could be translated by others as a mutual respect of force.

Farshem was not far from Bealby and several of the biker gangs from there decided it would be a shame to ignore the chance of instilling a little terror into the Friday night dances. Very soon 'The Assyrian came down like the wolf on the fold . . . ' The call to stand or fall had been made, and if we could bluff our way through this one we would not only save face but put ourselves in good standing behind a new shield. These stepping stones could only benefit our continued upwards climb. Saturday night was to be a show-down at Bealby, so with our six guns on we set out to confront the firepower of Farshem's leather hordes. Our intention was to survive and return intact.

Invigorated by the evening air we strode side by side through Bealby, our whistling combating any trepidation we might have felt about the evening's outcome. I loved to walk at night. There was no fear in this darkness, just gentle spaces of silence where lesser life slept undisturbed. The hunters of the night sky circled above us in graceful flight, dropping dramatically like falling arrows, their piercing marble eyes zeroing in with uncanny accuracy on helpless prey. Luck was never on the latter's side and any attempt to escape was outmanoeuvred by the lethal talons of the great grey owl as it plucked its victim from the ground and

97

bore it aloft with a victorious shriek. Triumphant, its heaving chest puffing proudly, it could be picked out illuminated by the searchlight of the moon.

Bealby really was a beautiful village and by day or night it never failed to leave an impression on me. Each one of the houses nestling comfortably together along the sloping road was a masterpiece of rustic architecture. Even the homes built within the last two decades were sculptured into character without putting as much as a blemish on the sense of continuity. Grey-stoned and thatched, they sat in ideal settings and one could imagine the hands of time sewing together these statesmen of a bygone era. Here was a craftsmanship no longer called for in a century of chrome and steel. These were monuments to an ancient trade intertwined with wistaria and winter jasmine. Their lawns were cushioned carpets of pure Lincoln green surrounded by thick orchards and floral beds of rhododendrons. Rock gardens with unlimited quantities of fragile blossom burst forth under the nurturing sun. At the crest of the hill Bealby's fourteenth-century church stood like a sentinel gazing with protective pride across the village. It was in this church that Alfred Lord Tennyson and his brother Charles worshipped as young men. At one time Charles was curate here and the two brothers were residents of their uncle's estate, the famed Bayons Manor. Before the Manor was dynamited in 1964 to give way to modern farming techniques, it had stood in the valley where the River Slaten flows fresh from its source at Bully Hill. Bayons Manor must have been a sight to behold with its battlement house complete with barbican and drawbridge. Even to this day there are traces of the original earthwork dating back to its occupation by Odo, Bishop of Bayeux, half-brother of William the Conqueror. I wondered what the misty ghosts of these great warriors and wordsmiths made of all that now took place in the area where they once trod with stately grace. The music to which they once gavotted in their spacious halls had changed hands through the ages, becoming hauntingly reminiscent. Any spectres eavesdropping on this cool evening might have heard the gentle strain of Brian Jones's harpsicord drifting into the night air introducing a plaintive 'My sweet Lady Jane, when I see you again . . . ' The spirits were willing, for everything old is new again.

Light tumbled on to the street from the club's open doorway

and we could tell by the laughter from within that the evening was proving to be a success. The one attribute this hall had in its favour was character. The other youth clubs tended to be cold and impersonal but this one was rather inviting. There was a warm glow emanating from its embracing structure which always managed to take the chill off a cold evening. The lights were kept at a modest level, producing a tranquillizing effect on the 'eyes for each other only' couples. The exterior walls were a mixture of rough timber and grey-stone slabs while the inner area was lined with polished oak, from the lacquered floors and panelled window ledges to the sturdy crossbeams that supported the high, wide ceiling. Many hands had spent hours polishing and sweeping, their pride unappreciated by we of little caring.

Paying the cover charge we stepped into the convivial atmosphere, where I was immediately pounced on by Christine Bundy, a fourteen-stone Amazon with an obvious crush on me – 'crush' being the operative word, as this gargantuan was totally unaware of her own strength. Her greeting paralysed me in a grip of vice-like proportions. This was not a girl to be taken lightly, and rejection could have been a dangerous undertaking. The safest bet was to remain pleasant, escaping into the crowd the moment the opportunity arose. It was the aroma of a passing cheese sandwich that momentarily broke her concentration. Aided by this diversion, I darted into a hole in the crowd and disappeared up a back staircase leading to a narrow balcony overlooking the dance floor. I found the boys leaning over the rail surveying the swaying forms below. Recovering from Christine's death grip, I was beginning to dig the sounds – 'Now she gets her kicks in Stepney, not in Knightsbridge any more . . . ' – when I saw them!

Lounging on the stage at the end of the room were four figures of antagonism. I recognized two of them as being Digger and Karl Thomas, a couple of noteworthy punks from Farshem. Their reputation was exceeded only by their elder brother Red, who was far and away the most notorious Ted in the area. The others were unfamiliar to me but, judging by their primitive gestures, I presumed they were merely toadies to the higher ranks. This would truly be a test of our ingenuity, as we had not expected such noteworthy opponents. It would have been easy to remain in the gallery and deny the existence of the threat below, but in our hearts we knew there were those present who would love to see us leave with our tails between our legs. To have the white line of the highway run straight along our backs and brand us for ever was unthinkable. Four feathers would never fall into our hands. I hitched up my jeans and dug my thumbs deep into my belt loops, aiding my bravado and preventing my hands from trembling. Leading the way down the stairs I mouthed along with the music, *'Don't play with me 'cause you're playing with fire ... '* Yeah, sure!

There were key locations in which one felt important and anything in the vicinity of the musical source was deemed an ace area. The musical source in this instance was located roughly two feet from the imposing boot of Digger Thomas, the kind of thigh-high footwear that was successful in grinding small round pebbles into fine powder. In comparison my boots looked decidedly puny and shone with an embarrassing glow due to the hours of buffing I had bestowed upon them; time I now wished had been spent doing something useful like filing my teeth or piercing my nose. It was impossible to assess his build as he had on the most amazing amount of clothing. Over a string vest he wore his shirt, over his shirt a heavy cable-knit sweater, on top of this a denim jacket and a leather flying vest topped off by a blue donkey jacket and several scarfs. How he could stand the heat I had no idea, for although it was chilly outside, in here it was roasting. He looked ridiculous and it was this look of amusement on my face that first caught his brother's eye.

Time stopped and was encapsulated in an instant of frozen terror as Karl's eyes bored through my skull and uprooted my nerve endings. Even in this unhinged state I could not help but think how much Karl Thomas resembled a sly fox, the kind of cunning caricature Beatrix Potter might design. The charming aggressor with gracious smile and cruel heart, whose dark narrow eyes were set in a slim feline face that was not so much unattractive as unnerving; whether he might kiss you or kill you was in his mind alone.

As I contemplated this literary assessment, the edges of Karl's mouth creased into a smile, doing little to put me at ease. The smile before you die! To make matters worse, the hypnotic trance cast upon me by this fox caught the attention of one of his underlings. Feeling our presence in this immediate area repre-sented a threat, he hunched his shoulders and pushed himself off the lip of the stage. His act of machismo was well executed and would have been quite effective had he not landed on Christine Bundy's foot, making her drop her plate of *petits fours*. Adding insult to injury, he made the fatal mistake of laughing as opposed to apologizing and was rewarded by a lethal blow to the side of the head from a large handbag. In the aftershock his head rebounded as if connected to a buoyant spring. His pompadour collapsed, dispersing a shower of Brylcreem, the slick wet strands slapping his face in retribution.

Karl looked on in impartial amusement as his friend's ego was deflated and left in ruins. Christine's perfectly executed clubbing had broken the tension, sending out the message that posturing was not just inherent in us, but proof perfect in the almost weeping Ted before our eyes. His companions remained insensitive to his predicament, for it was obvious his actions had embarrassed them. In order to cover himself Karl tossed off a disparaging remark towards his whimpering friend, slipped off the stage and moved towards us. He did well to read our eyes, for no longer did terror dwell within us. With the combined body weight of Steve and Eddie to support me he obviously saw the writing on the wall and, to give him his due, he maintained the maximum of cool as he stood before us. Nothing was said as the fox smiled and pushed his way firmly between us, disappearing into the crowd.

This was a satisfying beginning for phase two. It was a slim victory but now we understood there was little difference in the fronts we rivals constructed. The wall they had built was of flesh and blood; we were doing exactly the same. From now on it would be easier to create beautiful lies we could all live.

Eight

The initiation to drinking at an early age is of cultural importance to any child raised in the north of England. In fact, British youth in general has a natural affiliation with intoxicating beverage and stands head and shoulders above the rest of the world in its extraordinary capacity for it. This is due in part to the public house, a heritage dear to the hearts of all manner of Englishmen. Any number of houses constituting a dwelling area and without a pub nestled in its bosom is tantamount to treason. Throughout history there has always been a tavern along the way. The footsore soldier and weary traveller have often sat and drank with merchant and mariner in inns of ill-repute or splendid isolation. English literature is studded with infamous outlaws, brilliant thinkers and black-hearted villains who have at one time or another graced the British tavern with their immortal lines. It was at the Admiral Benbow that Blind Pew pressed the black spot into the palm of Black Dog, and at the Spouter Inn that Ishmael found passage with the ill-fated Ahab. In Sherwood Forest, Robin Hood drank at the Black Boar, while Oscar Wilde and the Rhymers Club congregated in London's Cheshire Cheese. The list is endless. Samuel Pepys, Dick Turpin, Nell Gwyn and Jack the Ripper all found comfort in the public house.

It may be argued that other countries have their watering holes, but they would be hard-pressed to find in them the character that graces the English pub. The American saloon of the Old West is a shadow of its former self, a spirit that has ceased to exist. What remains are millions of blue-collar bars of equal design strung out across the length and breadth of the United States. Even the gaiety of the Parisian café focuses far more on the artistic pioneer and consumptive poet sipping *absinthe*. When an Englishman enters a pub he goes in for one purpose, to drink – anything else is secondary. It is an institution unchanged, hallowed ground for the connoisseur of true ale.

One explanation for the Englishman's pursuit of inebriation and its attraction to the under-age is that the pub is believed to be the first true step to manhood. For us, it was the next logical progression from youth clubs and village-hall dances. In the limited confines of rural life we were for ever in hot pursuit of our elders, always eager to sample forbidden fruit.

The first time I was ever in a pub was not to quench my thirst, but to give a recital. At the age of eight I had been inadvertently spirited into a popular local under the coat-tails of a friendly farmer and, after causing a minor disturbance, was hoisted on to the bar to sing 'Barbara Allen' to a bunch of drunken navvies. My reward was nothing more than a few pence and a small shandy. I was saddened by the fact that I had not been initiated into the brew, but took comfort in the knowledge that it was my first taste of showbiz.

The pungent smells of casual recreation simply oozed out of the surroundings and the short time spent within these walls was enough to intoxicate me without the aid of beer. When the smell of stale booze and cigarettes becomes more tantalizing than the perfumed rooms in the palaces of kings, it is safe to presume you will spend more time in the bar than in the ballroom. The cosiness of the conversation, mingling with the laughter and ribald humour of the regulars, sent a tingling thrill up and down my spine. It was the living room of which I had always dreamed. Lead and oak married together in drowsy bliss, settled in their ways and lulling the patrons into a state of well-being. A jovial landlord lost among his pumps and glasses was berated by a crowd anxious to be replenished when last orders were called. At that moment I was prone to wish the years away between then and my coming of age.

Of course I didn't wait that long and it was three years short of my eighteenth birthday when the boys and I began to sidle into the bar, hidden in the hulking shadows of our older friends. At first our drinks were ordered for us so as not to afford the landlord a good look at our under-age features. We paid through the nose for this pleasure, for in order to obtain drinks for

103

ourselves we were obliged to get everyone else's, a sort of alcoholic blackmail. It was not as hard as it seemed, as the laws were lax in the majority of country pubs and a blind eye was turned if you acted accordingly to the rules of the house. In a healthy crowd it was possible to remain anonymous, making escape easy should the local constabulary pop in. The regulars viewed our presence with great amusement and usually encouraged us to indulge a little more than we were prepared for. Although we may have been the butt of their jokes, it was always these old fellas who would caution us to 'hoppit' if the law were about.

Before long our attitudes complemented our surroundings and we found acceptance in the pubs we frequented. We had the landlords' trust and that was important. It was up to us to control our actions and remain aware of our duty to duck out at the right moment. All the doors were open and with our first beer at the bar we entered a new phase. It was hard to imagine that heaven was anything less than a brown ale in a tall glass.

There was no way I could have got away with this in my own village. It would have been impossible to appear in the Dog & Cat in Doramby, the closest pub to home. Besides being incredibly uncomfortable, it would have been extremely unwise and not two seconds before my father would have found out. Whether or not my dad would have approved is food for thought. Even if he wasn't against me partaking of the odd pint, the thought of his fifteen-year-old son drinking in the local boozer might have caused him some embarrassment.

It was the Temple Arms in Market Slaten that we chose as our regular haunt. Besides being a safe distance from home, it was centrally located and drew a larger and livelier crowd. The Temple comprised a public bar, lounge area and snooker room. Because it was the most discreet and contained the best atmosphere, the latter became our favourite. It was here that the old hustlers gathered to rack 'em up on an impressive full-sized table, and without a doubt it was in this room that I fell full tilt into my rebellious years. Recognized notoriety, the favours of hard friends, and a relative attraction for girls caused my head to swell with an unhealthy pride. In true tradition I lost my way in a snooker hall and, although I never reached the stage of hardened criminal, I lost sight of life's true values and fell upon stony ground.

I'm a juvenile product of the working class
whose best friend floats at the bottom of a glass.

Webster's New English Dictionary describes delinquency as 'conduct that is out of accord with accepted behaviour or the law' emphasizing that it is a 'state of social or psychological maladjustment rather than criminal intent'. Had I known this at the time, I most likely would have been rather upset at being referred to as psychologically maladjusted, more so still if I had known what it meant. Yet there was no denying that my social conduct was balanced precariously on the borderline of the law. Had the four of us been in a Fifties' teenage 'B' feature, it would have been cinematic type-casting to call us juvenile delinquents. I try not to blame it on the booze; it just seems that the two went in tandem.

It's a well known fact that most kids have indulged in a little shoplifting in their time. Why not, it's all a part of growing up. What they may not have done is take the theory literally and lift an entire shop: lock, stock and barrel, building and all. Now, before you picture us as a rural wrecking crew dismantling Tesco's, let me explain. There were two general stores in Bramby. Deary's, the main one, was a legitimate building containing the staples necessary for the everyday running of the home. Catering to the needs of the community, it would go out of its way to accommodate all requests. It was an industrious operation run efficiently by Beryl Deary, an attractive spinster who, with her large and loyal assistant Maggie, worked hard to keep the people happy, right down to the most indecisive five-year-old clutching a sweaty threepenny bit at the sweet counter.

In total contrast to Deary's was Brown's. This bastion of lesser fundamentals was little more than a converted chicken hut on four wheels with a few shelves and a counter built into it. It sold cigarettes, sweets, tea, coffee and various household goods. Mrs Brown herself lived in a small grey house trapped between Small's Garage and Ben's Electrical Repairs. In order to purchase anything one had to knock on the door of her house to get her to open the shop. It was a quaint and permanent fixture in the

105

village and did a steady, if not roaring, trade. Most of this came from farm labourers dropping in for cigarettes and lemonade, or small children dragging her out in the pouring rain for a gumball and a penny chew. I remember standing outside her door for what seemed like an eternity trying to pluck up the courage to knock, as it always appeared to me that she resented the intrusion. It seemed that this dumpy little shack on its four fragile wheels was destined to remain in place till domesday; that is until one night in a funk of boredom I suggested to the lads that we attempt a little breaking and entering.

That night under cover of darkness we made our way through the village, blending into the shadows with criminal panache. Our intention was to prise open what we imagined would be a feeble lock and help ourselves to a few packs of ciggies. We were heavy smokers undaunted by yellow fingers and warnings of lung cancer. The anti-smoking lobby was still in its infancy and such scares were small fish compared to the prizes obtained with cigarette coupons. Like a million char-ladies throughout Britain, we were desperate to claim our toasters before our lungs collapsed.

Unfortunately what we found on arrival did not constitute easy pickings, and threaded cunningly through the latch was a sturdy length of chain secured by a large padlock. After inspecting this obstacle for several minutes, it became apparent to us that in order to remove it we risked the danger of being overheard. An English village at night is akin to a crater on the moon. The silence is so intense that the crack of a twig can be heard a hundred yards away, so you can imagine what a hacksaw and hammer on a length of chain might do. I don't know whose bright idea it was, but one of us suggested removing the chocks from under the wheels and rolling the store out of earshot. This was not easy, as over the years these devices had become lodged tightly and were loath to relinquish their position. Hindered by the moon's failure to cooperate, this endeavour took some time, as we had come totally unprepared for this inconvenience and it was necessary to keep striking matches in order to monitor our progress. In due time we succeeded and, with the last obstacles removed, set to rolling the stubborn hut from its position. This took a little muscle but, with the four of us lending our shoulders, we managed to heave it gently from its resting place and roll it down the short incline to the side of the road.

Our intention was to push it down the street on to the grounds of an abandoned house some fifty yards away and here, amid the soundproofing of trees, prise open the lock without detection. If all else failed, we could take a couple of planks off the side with a crowbar which, if we'd used our heads, might have been infinitely simpler. Being equally as thick as the aforementioned planks, we went about it the hard way and began trundling our prize down the road. As we approached our intended hiding place I constructed an impressive torch by wrapping my handkerchief around a fallen tree limb. In the darkness beyond the gates this would save us from a constant stream of matches slowly burning away the tips of our fingers. Reaching our destination, the boys took a breather and I turned from the wind to light the torch. With all eyes on the igniting at hand, no one heard the slow rumble of ancient wheels until the slow rumble became a small thunder, at which point we turned to see Mrs Brown's shop picking up speed and rapidly descending Pump Hill. What we had failed to realize was that the site to which we had manoeuvred our loot happened to be the brow of Bramby's steepest hill. With shrieks of realization we took off in hot pursuit in a vain attempt to stem the tide of impending doom. I was off like a shot, leading the pack like some derelict Olympian torch-bearer, holding aloft my flaming brand. By the time we reached the runaway it had picked up tremendous speed and all we could do, save throwing ourselves under the wheels, was hang on and hope we could steer it clear of disaster at the bottom of the hill.

On the way down we overtook several cars and I couldn't help picturing the late-night confrontation and the distraught drivers trying to convince their wives they had almost collided with a runaway chicken coop bright with flame and hell-bent on destruction. For all our screams and frantic pleading with the gods, nothing seemed to deter the impending collision course on which we were bound. Before us like some inviting giant stood the wide girth of an enormous oak tree. This seemed a logical time to abandon ship and, as much as we desired to dismount, the same fear magnetized our hands in a death grip on the shop. When we struck the tree it was as if the world had ended. Like a sick bull colliding with a concrete matador, the shop disintegrated and we were ejected into space. Hurled torch and all, like a dying comet I came to rest in a stagnant pool, my flame extinguished by a shower of frogspawn and slime. Emerging like a swamp monster I surveyed the damage. All around lay the remains of our destruction amidst which were sprawled the graceless forms of my companions, each one taking inventory on his self to ensure all was still intact. The impact had left us all at odds with our equilibrium, and unsteadily we wobbled off as best we could away from imminent discovery by approaching headlights.

This incident caused some fuss in the village, but after some minor investigation it was eventually forgotten. Mrs Brown seemed quite unperturbed by the loss of her livelihood and possibly looked on it as an omen, a gentle tap on the shoulder from those in the know that maybe it was time to retire. Now she could take comfort in the fact that no longer would 'Coronation Street' be rudely interrupted for a packet of Parkies and a Penguin.

This experience did nothing to curb our criminal ways and one evening, while strolling through Doramby, we noticed an open padlock hanging on the door of a large garage; possibly another situation by which we might benefit from someone's careless behaviour. After taking a quick look around to ensure that we were not being watched, the four of us filed in. It was dark inside but there was enough moonlight filtering in from the skylight to recognize immediately Phil McVee's grocery van. Phil and his wife had been the proprietors of the local fish and chip shop, but had given it up and opened a small shop down the street. In addition Phil had begun mobile service to the outlying villages by means of the large white truck that stood before us. I was well aware that no one ever locked their front door around here but to leave one's place of business unlocked and unattended was tempting fate. The thought of this made me feel positively guilty for all of sixty seconds, as a tiny wave of compassion passed through my conscience for a fleeting moment and was gone. Phil's generosity astounded me; not only had he left the back door of the truck open, he had been kind enough to provide us with a large torch which hung on the wall close by. Cigarettes were our main haul followed by chewing gum and chocolate bars. The interior was a little cramped so we took turns rifling the shelves. It all seemed too easy, a sort of pilfering for the simple, and I was surprised there weren't little arrows on the wall along the street proclaiming, 'Phil McVee's van this way, help yourself!'

This became a routine and, whenever we were low on smokes, one or two of us would nip down to Phil's van to replenish our supply. We never did get caught, but Steve and I came close one night when Phil came down to the garage to work on his car while we were inside helping ourselves. With our hearts in our mouths and bladders in despair, we were forced to lie face down on the floor of the van while Phil changed his transmission fluid. It may have taken only ten minutes, but to us it seemed like he was building the car from scratch. The phantom of fear floated over us doing all it could to give the game away, tickling our noses, dusting our throats and encouraging us to fart in terror. We held out and on our return treated Rick and Eddie to an elaborate story of cunning and deceit, which I'm positive neither of them believed but no doubt enjoyed.

Occasionally we would return from one of our excursions with a tin of Campbell's Cream of Tomato, throw it into a saucepan and heat it up on the Primus. This would take place in the Old House which by now had become our recreation centre. We had made the place quite cosy with a few armchairs, some knick-knacks, mostly knicked, and an old record player complete with warped and scarred forty-fives. Dusty, Sandie and Cilla looked down on us from the walls, their glossy teeth forced into permanent smiles patronizingly endorsing all we did. We treasured this refuge from society and spent hours here planning the weekends, discussing trends and the technique of female conquest. It became the hub of our unity, a war room where we would synchronize our minds before setting out to colour the night.

> *Being wiry and thinking loudly*
> *about the things sent to make you move . . .*

Back in class, the fifth year of school turned out to be as pleasant as I had expected as we chose our classes with a pin and manoeuvred lethargically between lessons. There was little else to teach us now. The rudimentary triple Rs had been duly logged in our brains and beyond that the teaching staff felt their efforts were in vain. It seemed the transition from scholar to wage earner was of little interest to them. We had passed this way before and we would again, a faceless train of adolescents trooping through to be dipped in ink and stamped on to the growing register of arrivals and departures. In that last year we lived the life of the lotus-eaters, whittling wood, making ashtrays and stools, or daubing hieroglyphic symbols on large canvases, creating art like anthropoids. We would skip class and slip out of the gates when we felt the claustrophobia of knowledge was too much for us. Often during these illegal recesses we could be found around the corner at a pal's house picking the lock on his father's liquor cabinet and downing a couple of vodkas before the next class. During the weekly cross-country, Danny and I would normally peel off from the pack and into the Temple for a quick pint and a game of snooker.

Under this liberal regime I lost touch with many of the impulses that had once spurred me to enjoy creative thinking. I had no time for these now. I had burned the broom on which I rode to the heights of my own imagination. Those designs were a lost cause locked away with my childhood toys. The noble knights had fallen off the page, their armour rusted by the changing tide as the restless age engulfed me. The magician inside had been replaced by the ogre who craves the golden goose. If only I could have retained some semblance of that spark which propelled my innocence, for there was no harm in the things I now desired, only in the excess to which I desired them. To balance the old and the new would have been bliss, but to sever the head of adolescence as I did was a shame. As Bob Dylan said, *'Time will tell just who has fell and who's been left behind.'*

There was one instance when I regained a little of my old compassion for art as an alternative to manual labour; this being the time we were dispatched to see the local youth employment officer, an experience that was enough to douse the flame of anyone with one iota of individuality. His name was Mr Matlock and he occupied space in the local council building. Council buildings are depressing enough in any light, but to go there and be interrogated on the basis of one's intelligence was a situation of infinite distaste. When my turn came I was fully prepared to give a good account of myself. Even if my schoolwork was not the most impressive, I was sure I could charm him into believing

110

there might be more to this boy than meets the eye. Going so far as to dress to impress, I secured my tie in a fashionable Windsor and brushed my blazer until it was lint-free. I was shepherded into his office by a sour secretary who looked upon my presence as the arrival of a disease.

Although the room was small, it was hard at first to locate any sign of life, as clouds of sickly-smelling blue smoke occupied every square inch. This, I surmised, came from a large brier pipe clenched firmly between my inquisitor's teeth. Without looking up he motioned me to sit. After several minutes he raised his head and I detected immediately that this was a man not in love with his job. He wore it like a weight around his shoulders, a responsibility thrown upon him by a merciless world. Seeing him sitting there in his heavy tweeds with a trickle of sweat tracing down his furrowed brow would have killed the confidence of Adolf Hitler. In a weary monotone he recited what I imagine was his stock speech about the responsibility we owed our teachers and how they had worked hard to establish a place for us in society; how, when we returned home with our first wage packet, we could look proudly into our mothers' eyes and say, 'From now on, Mum, I'm paying you back for all you've done to raise me right.' It was enough that I had to refrain from gagging on his pipe smoke, but with the delivery of this drivel I was really ready to puke.

In asking me what I wished to pursue in life he was decidedly small in his thinking and had an extraordinary knack of killing any conversation that dealt with my desires. For the most part he was concerned with what elements of farmwork most appealed to me and what position was best suited to me in working the land. Was it to be animals or agriculture? Did I foresee driving a tractor or shovelling shit out of a chicken coop? What I foresaw at that particular moment was an end to him shovelling this shit out to me. For Christ's sake, what was all this farm talk? I hadn't even mentioned farming, so why the hell was he bothering to inquire about my agricultural preferences? He was visibly taken aback when I did manage to get a word in edgeways to inform him of my absolute disinterest in the subject. I was aware that the majority of my peers preferred this profession and looked forward to following in their fathers' gumboots, but I thought it presumptuous to expect that what the majority wished for was

111

necessarily what we all dreamed of. I didn't want to be a brain surgeon, I just wanted someone to listen sympathetically and suggest possible ways I might achieve a more adventurous profession. No go! If I expected sympathy of any kind from this clone, what I got was the sympathy of a jailer for a condemned man. Don't rock the boat, don't change the system. Figures and columns say you are of the percentage that tills the soil. It was the brick-wall syndrome and I could feel that whatever I said was going to be interpreted as anarchy. However, I did have the audacity to convey my desire to attain a job on one of the local newspapers. With a great deal of harumphing, a visibly shaken Mr Matlock dismissed me, promising to get back to me at a later date. Feeling that I had won a minor victory in the moral battle with authority, I cut my way through a cloud of St Bruno, giving his archaic secretary a knowing wink on the way out.

With my job prospects in the hands of a buffoon and the languid pace of school's last term, I had an abundance of time in which to contemplate romance. The dating department had been through a major crisis lately due in part to the termination of my relationship with Daphne, which died a natural death. She felt the time I spent with my friends could be put to better use, the better use in question being the region between her neck and navel. It was a complaint not unfounded, but the prospect of biking twenty miles every weekend for a limited fumble on the couch was not sufficient reward for such a sacrifice. I tried it several times and arrived irritable and unaroused. I didn't like the pressure and most of all I didn't enjoy the agony of pedalling up the steep hills that led to her amorous embrace. The final straw came in the guise of Rick, Steve and Eddie who turned up uninvited one Sunday while Daph and I were in the midst of heavy petting. Oblivious to Daphne's obvious annoyance, they set about making sandwiches, rearranging her record collection and relieving themselves, doing anything in fact that might restrict her advances on me. Once they had emptied both the refrigerator and their bladders, they threw me my jacket and informed her I had to be going. Seeing my predicament, it was obvious that my friends were terminating my relationship for me. Daphne's frosty goodbye was to be the last one I received from her doorstep, my first great romance now a thing of the past.

Not long after this incident I hooked into a winner, a catch that made me the envy of my contemporaries. Nikki Quick was an infamous blonde-haired grammar school girl notorious for her string of boyfriends. While not unattractive, it was her personality that made her the most desired female in the area. Other girls regarded her as a tart and called her a common floozy behind her back, concocting stories of her moral conduct so exaggerated that they made Mary Whitehouse look like Mata Hari. There was no doubting she got around and had dated some rather notorious local rebels. It was even rumoured she had been involved at one time with the drummer of the Casuals, Lincoln's top band. It wasn't hard to detect that jealousy was the motivation for most of the stories about her; she was, after all, achieving what the other girls wished for, namely notoriety. All this gossip only worked to her advantage, making her seem more desirable, mysterious and deliciously bad. She had friends everywhere and became a status symbol on the pillion of any biker in favour, a sort of Betty Grable of the local armed forces.

Nikki lived with her very liberated mother in a council cottage on the main road into Market Slaten. Aware of her existence long before the boys and I had infiltrated Slaten's pub and café life, I had seen her from the school bus walking into town, swinging her satchel provocatively. During lunch breaks Danny and I watched as she flitted in and out of the Waterloo Café, the buttons on her blouse undone to within an inch of decency and her grey pleated skirt shifting seductively around her thighs. She was constantly in the company of those older than herself, intimidating anyone in my own age group from approaching her. Things now being the way they were, the boys and I were in a position of visibility, and within a short time it was obvious that she was aware of our presence. Normally we drew an attentive crowd in the lounge area of the Temple, a group made up of girls from my class at school and several older factory girls who had become close friends. Between the Temple and the Waterloo it was inevitable that Nikki and I would fall in step with each other. After all, we both had an image to maintain, so it was destiny that the two greatest exponents of self-promotion should ultimately be drawn to one another.

Nikki was, in a word, irresistible. Good-hearted, free-spirited and simply fun to be with, she had no cares and complained about nothing. If this was the vamperella who caused venom to flow from the mouths of other girls, then it was indeed a sad state of affairs, for in maligning Nikki they were using their own insecurities as weapons to combat something that didn't exist. What they perceived as immoral behaviour was nothing more than a spirit imbued with happiness. I really liked old Nik; she was totally compatible, fitting in with my friends and never complaining in their presence. Their respect for her was mutual and she came to be regarded as the sister member of the pack, our very own Lady d'Artagnan.

She was also instrumental in our introduction to Red Thomas, the legendary elder brother of our Bealby Youth Club adversaries. Red was a force to be reckoned with, a small-town hoodlum with a big reputation, most of it self-inflicted. He was slight and pale with a dangerous look which I imagined to be his ace in the hole. With Red in our pocket we reached a new zenith. Our sense of gypsy ideology appealed to him and he took us under his wing like a benevolent godfather.

Besides boys, the other love in Nikki's life was music and it was this subject that initially sparked off our relationship. She adored to dance, and with the help of Buddy Holly she taught me to jive. Jiving was still big in the provinces and although it was 1965, there seemed some doubt about it in the Lincolnshire time warp. Nikki had definite leanings towards bikes and grease but was surprisingly hip to current musical trends. With the exception of her tastes in dancing and rocker rhetoric, she totally adored James Brown, Otis Redding and Bob Dylan, all of whom were still enjoying cult status. The Dylanesque image appealed to her, and I think in the boys and me she sensed some of that spirit we were so desperate to achieve. I charmed her with my philosophy and impressed her with my poetry, although my philosophy was opinionated and of limited scope and my poetry juvenile, rambling and without form. The product of too many 'Twilight Zones', the settings for my poems were usually barren landscapes where little hope remained. In these sagas of survival my characters were hopeless souls caught in the aftermath of nuclear holocausts; dark and brooding, they foresaw little hope for a civilization strangled by political greed. Conjuring up Orwellian nightmares, I created faceless dictators whose goon squads stalked through a decaying suburbia in search of subversive societies. They were on the whole without thought, but not without merit.

If I plagiarized it was unintentional, as plagiarism was an act of which I was incapable. The images were my own and I could not steal what I did not know. After all, youthful pretension was the order of the day. Were we not on the eve of a new age? I was merely preaching what was popular; it may have been badly written and ignorant of the true facts, but it was hipper than hell. I was certainly posing no threat to the true gurus of doom, I was merely an amateur fanatic.

My work, however, was not altogether inane. At one point Nikki had commissioned me to ghostwrite some verse for her school magazine which ultimately won her first prize in their poetry contest. I went so far as to bind my collected works together under the heading of 'Goliath', a *double entendre* title I imagined to be rather clever; the Goliath in question representing his biblical self as well as the tyrannical giants of evil that loomed over the world threatening the peace of mankind. I'm sad to say this historic volume vanished with the years, leaving the time capsules of tomorrow free from my prophetic gems.

Will the things we wrote today sound as good tomorrow?

Meanwhile in the realms of reality, the boys and I figured it was time to show a little hospitality and open our clubhouse to our growing circle of friends. The Old House, which had now been christened the 'White Rhino', for God knows what reason, was experiencing a major overhaul. We scrubbed, dusted, rearranged the furniture and painted the front door shocking-pink. The sound system had been serviced and the records replaced in their correct jackets. To acquire a moody nightclub effect we replaced the existing lightbulbs with soft coloured ones. Soon the place was looking like a cross between grandma's parlour and a pre-war Nazi whorehouse, the perfect balance of rustic charm and decadent comfort. Proud of their accomplishment, the Restoration Committee decided to celebrate with a party.

News of this coming event spread like wildfire and before long our wing-ding had become the premier topic of conversation throughout the area. Unfortunately there was one slight problem.

What we had here was a relatively small dwelling and not the Albert Hall, which we could have filled had all who wished to attend done so. The whole affair began to get rather ugly when rumours of forced entry reached our ears. These threats were laid to rest with the intervention of Red Thomas, who for the price of a bottle of scotch promised to police the event, warding off any gate-crashers. Comfortable in the knowledge that we had our very own guardian angel hovering close at hand, we set to finalizing the guest list and arranging last-minute details. Parties then were basic affairs and anyone expecting canapés or things on sticks had to forget it; here they'd be lucky to get a bag of crisps. It was, to put it bluntly, a matter of booze and birds with a bit of idle chatter slung in for good measure. Everyone was asked to bring a bottle, although we did manage to provide a good bar which was accomplished by thieving fingers and pooled resources.

The turnout that night was substantial with many of our female guests being bused in by a concerned contingent of parents. There were the Hempton and Bealby crowds along with folks from Market Slaten and Woolworth; even Daphne put in an appearance to show there were no hard feelings. Sensibly the girls outnumbered the boys, as we weren't very good at sharing, and many of the males in attendance were basically there to balance the books. The local village kids whom I rarely saw any more hung around outside watching the crowds arrive and hoping to be invited in. The problem was not that they weren't welcome, but that there were those among them with whom we had poor relations, and indeed several who disliked us intensely. Whether they regarded me as a traitor for associating with outsiders I'm not sure, but in order to maintain the status quo, I felt it necessary to keep them all at arm's length. With Red off his leash I felt we were perfectly safe from an invasion of any kind.

It was quite an event, as it was not often that our guests got to attend a party in such an atmosphere of independence. Normally these affairs took place in the home with the parental eye constantly surveying the proceedings to make sure the behaviour of the guests remained within the boundaries of decency. Here at the White Rhino there was none of that to worry about, no one to tell you to get your feet off the furniture (we didn't have any), no one constantly pushing ashtrays under your nose (we didn't have

116

any), and no one complaining if a glass got broken (we didn't have any of those either). It was a situation constructed purely for the party animal. So with the Kinks blasting out of the speakers and the boys and I spiffed out in our best party duds, there seemed little to distract us from revelling in the orgy of our own design. It was certainly not an orgy in the biblical sense, but to those of us still on the threshold of complete sexual abandonment it seemed risqué enough. My parents were surprisingly lenient and went so far as to leave the front door open so that anyone needing to use the toilet could do so. Lord knows what they must have made of the procession of chattering *femmes* teetering down the hallway pockmarking the parquet and filling the air with cheap scent. As the evening progressed, the confident approach of the guests down the same hallway became less sure-footed, until the strut became a stumble ending up in a desperate crawl to reach the bathroom in time.

Half-way through the party I was upstairs firmly rooted in an overstuffed armchair enjoying the charms of the equally overstuf-fed Nikki, when Eddie appeared to inform me that my inebriated ex was causing a disturbance below. After consuming a liberal quantity of vodka and lime, Daphne had commandeered the record player and was constantly spinning Jerry Lee Lewis's 'How's My Ex Treating You'. This masochistic display of self-indulgence for Nikki's benefit was beginning to annoy the other guests who were on the verge of breaking the record over her head. Detesting this sort of confrontation, I didn't wish to wade in and reprimand her, but with everyone expecting me to do so I saw no other choice. By the time I got downstairs she had reached the belligerent stage and was beginning to swing, so the chance of a subtle solution seemed out of the question. All eyes were upon me as I moved in to do battle with the woman scorned. Through bleary eyes she caught sight of my approach and began to hurl a torrent of sarcasm in my direction. Her conduct was far from lady-like and it appeared impossible to talk to her as such. Before she embarrassed me further I grabbed her and threw her over my shoulder, causing her to vomit down by back. Disgusted, I loosened my grip, letting her slide from my shoulder to land comatose upside-down on her head. More concerned with changing my shirt, I left her in the centre of the room, her skirt slipping slowly down around her head, her legs erect and her knickers on display. The party continued around her, the revellers content that Jerry Lee was history.

Returning through the garden with a fresh shirt and *l'amour* on my mind, I heard the muffled sound of violent behaviour coming from the side of the house. Fearing one of my guests had got into a fight with a local, I rushed into the Rhino and enlisted Steve's help. If there was indeed a scuffle outside then it was not my intention to die alone. With my unenthusiastic companion backing me up, we wove our way stealthily towards the sound of the disturbance. Silhouetted before us in the moonlight was not the vicious brawl we expected, but a solitary guest thumping the sap out of a small apple tree. The antagonist in this case was the Amazonian Christine Bundy's younger brother, Paul. Paul, whose exercises in physical prowess were normally concentrated on impressing us, had always been keen to infiltrate the pack but had never quite made the grade. We had taken him along occasionally but his personality didn't match up to the standards by which we operated, and at this precise moment he was in the process of making a right Charlie of himself. Pissed beyond belief, he had mistaken the harmless tree for an unwanted guest and was involved in fighting a losing battle with it. He turned and gazed unsteadily at our approach, his eyes illuminated with passion. Seeing us, he backed off with his guard up, his bloody fists sparring with the night air. Steve and I looked on sympathetically as he tried vainly to impress us, bouncing around the tree, throwing punches at his stationary opponent. It was not an easy task telling him he was doing battle with a tree, as his grunting attack and pleas for assistance made this information inaudible. Between abusive taunts he would demand if the tree had had enough. Obviously it had, for his next stroke dislodged a large apple which was deposited right between his eyes, a knockout that constituted a win by shock alone. We carried his body back to the Rhino and laid him next to my unconscious ex on the lawn outside. As the night progressed the area began to look like Boot Hill as the over-indulgent were laid to rest side by side.

In the course of the evening there were several other incidents that kept me from the pursuit of Nikki's virtue. Eddie's performance of crawling on his knees down the hallway to the

118

bathroom and clawing on the door in search of the handle amused my parents, until he found it and fell through, to land face first between the feet of a squatting female. Then there was the small fire that might have consumed us all – had I not discovered brown ale doubles nicely as a fire extinguisher – this being due to some brilliant specimen attempting to use the arm of the couch as a candleholder. Dealing with drunken minds was not easy, for as the night passed I was rapidly reaching Mach One in my flight to Utopia. By the end of the evening it seemed we had survived, as the remnants were transported off heaving heavily from the windows of their fathers' cars. The only footnote to our successful evening was Eddie, the last to leave and the worst for wear. He fell off his bike somewhere between Bramby and Spridillby, crawled into a field and fell asleep, only to be awoken the next morning as he was nearly ploughed into the ground by an oncoming tractor.

I'm a genuine example of a social disease.

———————————

There was definitely some needle involved whenever the boys and I attended dances at Temple Lord, the grammar school to which I had miserably failed to gain entry. Not so for my brother, who had carved himself a fine career at this institute, excelling in sports and athletics as well as in everyday studies. He was a well-liked student, popular with both his classmates and teachers, his only disability in his years at this prominent school being his younger brother. Our undeniable relationship by blood was not something he wished to ackowledge, and it seemed that the reputation I savoured so much was not one respected by the grammar school sect. Within the ranks of Temple Lord's trendies and scholastic brainboxes, the lads and I were regarded as heathen rabble. Upon discovery of our relationship, he would be grilled on the problems in our home that might allow a bad seed like me to exist.

So it was with great pride that I listened to his abortive attempts to steer me away from functions held upon Temple Lord's sacred ground. This excommunication hurt me deeply: to be branded a black sheep by my brother was one thing, but to be thought of as a deviate by a bunch of squeaky-clean bookworms was a glove thrown in my face. Naturally we attended every function, made everyone thoroughly uncomfortable and on several occasions were ejected for bad behaviour. I embarrassed my brother literally to the point of tears, his frustration made worse by the open signs of affection I heaped upon him in full view of his friends.

The dances were on the whole very enjoyable and when we were allowed to, we managed to have a good time. Part of the problem stemmed from our appearance. Most of the guys were 'modded' out to the hilt, while we were the cause of stares of distaste in our stencilled combat-jackets and studded Sam Browns. Our hair was long and unkempt, while theirs was piled into the backcombed coconut style favoured by the Small Faces and the Who. They wore stylish striped shirts with tab collars while we preferred faded denims. Our feet were our transportation and the clothes we wore represented protection as well as choice. Any action on their part to belittle us was unwise; we weren't violent but we were touchy. Luckily they kept their distance, as it was obvious they valued their clothes as well as the lacquered domes on top of their heads.

We began to travel more and more frequently by foot, thinking of it as more romantic. At weekends we would make excuses to our respective parents saying we were spending the night elsewhere. Instead we roamed the countryside visiting friends in distant villages and sleeping at night in barns and abandoned buildings. Another good spot in which to kip were the local sports' pavilions – most villages had one and they were generally well-maintained and reasonably insulated. In desperate times I was known to curl up in the occasional call box or sleep across the wheel inside a tractor cab, but in general we found somewhere a little more comfortable. We fought a constant battle with the cold, and a bottle of Scotch was always a comfort during the long winter nights beneath the straw. Why we chose to sleep in such discomfort when we could be safely tucked up in a warm bed is unknown. We never wished we were home beneath the sheets; on the contrary, we acted according to our feelings and were totally happy exploring in this way, content in the knowledge that at the end of it we had homes to return to. It showed a spirit of independence and if I did nothing else at this point to be proud of, at least no one could have accused me of complacency. For all its negative points, for us being on the road had an abundance of positives. We were country boys to the core and what better way to experience the changing seasons than walking through them with our eyes wide open.

In the daylight the fields unfolded before us and coveys of doves exploded from the trees at the sound of our approaching footfall. The grey morning sky split down the middle as the sun burst through illuminating the corn with a crown of gold. Hedgerows came alive with sound, a cacophony of creatures calling out to each other across the rich flat acres. We passed awakening farms and heard the lowing of cattle and the irritated crow of the rooster. Milk churns rattled and farm hands whistled, each one and everything in its way laying a hand upon the key that winds the world.

After dusk we walked upon a path lit only by the moon, our laughter echoing in the still of the night. Sobered by the chilly sting of the air we marched without regret, our breath hanging like tiny clouds above us. Then happy in our unity, we would lie in the hay with sacks across us as the hang-nail moon hovered above. We were never babes in the woods, only children in straw; irreverent angels in a cradle of haloes.

Nine

The reckless age was indeed upon us and what we lacked in the wisdom of Solomon we more than made up for in the restless hobo soul. Pilgrims in progress, we depleted our shoe leather with amazing regularity as the winding road became our home away from home. In the months that followed, my school days became a pillow on which to lay my head and rest in between bouts of malcontent and sorties into mayhem. Like the James Gang we were rapidly being blamed for each and every act of vandalism from Lincoln's city limits to the foot of the Wolds. There was certainly no point in us complaining; after all, it was a notoriety of our own choosing. We had made our bed and, for all our annoyance, it was there for us to lie in. The seeds we had sown had set the wheels in motion and, like Mrs Brown's shop, they were now running uncontrollably downhill. Naturally, we did nothing to apply the brakes.

There was a particular group of heavies whom we wished to impress in order to add one more notch to our protection agency. We were at this time accumulating guardian angels all the time, our motto being that safety was undeniably to be found in numbers. To cement our image of street toughs not to be messed with, we concocted a fable of sheer bravado guaranteed to reach their ears. There were dances held every weekend at Weaton, an RAF base on the top road to Lincoln, which were up-market affairs requiring the appendage of a jacket and tie to gain entry. These dos were not to be missed and if it meant conforming to company policy then who were we to question it. We did tend to feel a little awkward out of uniform but it was usually worth it in the long run.

The crowd was well-behaved and basically middle class, coming from the estates around Lincoln and the surrounding area. There were, of course, the Air Force brats, a snooty bunch with noses seemingly held aloft by imaginary fish-hooks. We were aware that those we wished to impress knew of these functions and their rules, although they would never dream of attending. For all their toughness they were not ready to tangle with the security of the armed forces.

One Sunday afternoon we arrived as usual at the Waterloo Café in Market Slaten. Sundays were big at the Waterloo, as everyone converged there to share their exploits of the previous evening. The motorbikes lined up outside forewarned us that the leather hordes were gathered inside and that, yet again, we must exorcise the demons of doubt in the limited minds of our adversaries. We pushed open the door and marched confidently in. Heads turned, jaws dropped and eyes rolled as a murmur of reverence rolled around the room like a languid wave. Before the stunned crowd, the four of us stood taped and bandaged, the obvious recipients of some terrible accident. Steve's hand was tightly bandaged and hung professionally in a neat sling, Rick and Eddie had plasters placed strategically about their faces, while I sported a rather splendid black eye-patch.

We were immediately assailed with questions as to how we had received such massive injuries, while those whom we hoped to impress sat silently in the corner simmering with interest. Not wishing to jump the gun, we refrained from spilling the beans, with a good-natured wave of our hands and a casual, 'Oh, it's nothing . . . I'm sure you'll hear about it soon.' Under pressure, however, we broke down, and as the flock pulled up their chairs I recounted with great modesty the altercation that had never happened the night before.

The four of us had decided to invade the sanctimonious confines of Weaton's reputedly groovy dance club. Of course we were not about to put on a jacket and certainly was there no way these boys would be caught wearing a tie. (There were spontaneous 'oohs' and 'aahs' and the sound of shifting chairs as I continued.) We had arrived in our normal attire as the event was in full swing. Couples were streaming in, tailor-made and pressed to order. Girls, attractive but stuck-up, looked us up and down in disgust as we tagged behind them, whistling and making suggestive remarks. (Guffaws and catcalls on cue from my captive audience.)

At the front door we were stopped by the outstretched palm of a large hand followed by, 'And where d'you think you're going, then?'

'Inside, chief,' says I.

'Not dressed like that you're not!' says he. (My audience is already under my spell.)

'And what's wrong with the way we're dressed?' says Eddie.

'It don't concur with regulation dress code, mate,' says this big bugger, taking a really stand-offish position.

'Oh, and what is regulation dress code, if I may ask?' says Rick, all sweet and innocent-like.

'Listen, you little smart-arse, if you want to get in here tonight you'd better piss off home and change into a suit and tie. Now bugger off!'

'Oh,' I says, 'It's a tie I need, is it?'

At this point I turn and make a gesture to Steve who comes over, walks up to this big bloke and says 'Do I need a tie too, mister?'

'Of course you need a bloody tie too, you all need bloody ties!'

Well, at this Steve whips out a big pair of kitchen scissors and snips off this bouncer's tie neatly beneath the knot.

'Now I've got one!' says Steve. 'Can I come in?'

(Heads automatically snap back. My audience is dumbfounded, riveted by our bravery. Out of the corner of my eye I can see it's working. I continue.)

Well, of course the first thing that happens is this bloke takes a swing at Steve. Steve's expecting this and steps back. The bloke misses and Steve follows through, landing a good hook on his kisser. It didn't do Steve's hand much good, but then it didn't do our bouncer too much good either. Reinforcements come teeming out and it looks like we're in big trouble.

(I pause for a gulp of tea; all this lying's making me thirsty. I go on.)

Well as it happens we were outnumbered, but we give a good account of ourselves, soil a few suits and leave with a few injuries.

I now stick my hand deep into my pocket. 'And enough ties for all of us!' I pull from my pocket an assorted collection of severed ties and hold them aloft like David displaying the head of Goliath. Our ovation is outstanding, major victory is on the cards.

We moved towards the object of this exercise to receive their praise and accept their allegiance, but as we closed in a look of sheer terror formed on their faces as they deflated in tandem. Hurriedly they scrambled from the table and fled through the side exit. We stared into the wake of their retreat, confused by their departure. It looked as if our plan had outstretched its boundaries and instead of respect we'd instilled fear and alienated a possible ally. The myth we were creating was getting out of control. Remaining undetected was now our number one priority; one slip and we would be strangled in a web of our own lies.

We'll kill the fatted calf tonight so stick around . . .

Occasionally on Saturdays we took the bus into Lincoln to do a little window-shopping. It ran three times a day through our village, taking about an hour to get from its starting point in Grinly, several miles south of Bramby, to the bus station in Lincoln. It skirted through Spridillby on its journey, saving my friends any additional foot-slogging. Buses were prompt and careered with deadly accuracy through a myriad of villages and winding country lanes *en route* to their destination. Making these detours wasn't unpleasant as the scenery, although far from spectacular, was not without charm. The Saturday bus normally picked up the womenfolk going in to do their shopping, the once-a-week trek into the city to stock up.

Among the other curios clambering aboard along the way might be a freshly scrubbed farmer reborn after his weekly tub and all ready for a rave-up. They normally sat subdued, cap in hand at the front of the bus, gazing placidly out of the window at the passing countryside, their boots polished to a high gloss and their threadbare tweeds patched many times at the elbows. A major contrast to the return journey later that evening, when they would stumble aboard the last bus home, well lubricated and lusting for the bus conductress. Beside this rural oddity, there was of course the occasional mawkish couple going into town for a big afternoon at the pictures and a swift Wimpy and chips at the local greasepit. She would hold her handbag in the crook of her arm and clasp her cardie firmly in front of her as he sat upright next to her in his best Burton suit and spit-curl. Both would stare vacantly ahead with a look of lasting despair, never a word passing between them.

We eyed these accessories with juvenile contempt and viewed them as flotsam on the sea of humanity. Our attitude towards these people was not favourable, as we saw in them a failure to rise above the norm. They were humdrum and boring, everything we wished not to be. We strove to rise above that lifestyle and never be caught compromising society's rules. Big dreams for such little people, only we never managed to see how small and insignificant we were in reality.

From an historical standpoint Lincoln is an impressive city, its origins stretching back more than 2,000 years. Long before Julius Caesar landed, there was a Celtic settlement situated at its highest point. Later the Romans built their military fortress on this site and called it *Lindum Colonia*, a garrison of major importance during their occupation. Between the Roman withdrawal and the Norman conquest, both Saxons and Danes took turns at controlling the area, each in their own way adding to both its architecture and growth. Alfred the Great installed a mint and much of the coinage depicting the early kings was struck here. A little under two years after the Battle of Hastings, William the Conqueror ordered the construction of Lincoln Castle, incorporating the structures left by its Roman predecessors.

In 1702 Bishop Remigius, who had accompanied William from Normandy, was appointed Bishop of Lincoln and set to building what is now the city's crowning glory. After twenty years of painstaking design and back-breaking labour they constructed what remains one of the finest cathedrals in this or any other land. Its majesty is breathtaking to behold and dwarfs any other flaws this thriving city may have acquired over the centuries. Below, it is busy and often congested, the old rubbing shoulders with the new, but atop the hill is an area untampered by progress. From every angle it is a salute to the past; narrow cobbled streets, tilting buildings with creaking timbered ceilings above rough-hewn stone. However, in our particular phase of plebeian cruising it was the cheap lure of progress that drew us to Lincoln.

We hit the routine shops, checking out the best bargains in

126

eccentric attire, army surplus being a great favourite. Anything in battle-green appealed to the commando in us and we spent hours lost among endless racks of camouflage and khaki. Our purchases were limited as our financial resources were of minor proportions. I recall one occasion when Eddie and I each saved for weeks to buy a pair of atrocious burgundy jeans with a white plastic belt. At the time we thought they were the cat's whiskers and no doubt so did everyone else, style and taste not being a rural commodity.

Flashes of colour were rare in the uniform of the day and, for the most part, while not on the level of Leningrad and Cracow, the North seemed to prefer a sombre approach to the brilliant world of *haute couture*. Whether this was a reflection of overcast skies or a tendency to uniformity I don't know, but for a people proud to voice their opinions and cling to empire status one might think we'd have tried a little harder.

One area in which we did excel back then in the mid-Sixties was rock and roll. Not even the United States, which was going through a musical drought during this period, could hold a candle to us. In fact, thanks to the British invasion, they were once more reaping the benefits of colonial aid. The record store was the one place I never missed; music was my communion and I received it like a holy order. I scanned the charts and leafed through the glossy LP covers protected by their plastic jackets stacked neatly in alphabetical order. I was still heavily entrenched in my white-man-sings-the-blues period, favouring the Animals and Them. The lead singer of Them was a leprechaunic Irishman called Van Morrison to whom Steve bore a remarkable similarity. Dylan still remained my Messiah, he could do no wrong. To me, he spoke like a generation in unison echoing the sentiments of a million faltered souls. The conviction with which he sang scorched and stung, shooting arrows from his guitar strings into the hearts of profiteers and politicians.

The other stop along the way of great importance was a newsagent's near the outdoor market next to the river. I remained an avid reader of pop magazines and this shop stocked them all on a regular basis. Cheaper than records, in some way they gave me as much pleasure. They didn't sing to me but did instil an almost carnal delight. I treasured them and handled them as if they were leather-bound first editions – ne'er crease nor fold was tolerated.

No day out in Lincoln would be complete without a visit to the A-1, arguably the finest fish and chips north of London. Cod and chips fit for a king, heaped with fat scraps and mushy peas. It was a dive of a place, tilting precariously forward on its foundations, creating the effect that at any moment it might fall forward into the Brayford which ran just feet from its front door. The patrons would lean over the railings at the side of the river, eating their fish suppers and tossing chips to the swans circling below. I imagine that many of these poor creatures satiated with fat floated upstream like a lard Armada to die along the way of cholesterol poisoning.

Chip shops in general were pretty good all through our county due, I imagine, to the fine fish landed nearby at Grimsby. The rancid smell of chip fat is inherent in every town from John O'Groats to Land's End, and in fact the only time one is truly aware of it is when it isn't there. It was warm food for the cold road and in my teenage years I made much use of a steaming fish and six wrapped in the *Daily Mirror*. It never tasted the same in anything but the tabloids; after all, it was the fuel for the furnace, the mainstay of the working man.

At the end of the afternoon we headed for the bus station in order to catch the five o'clock home. The interlude between our arrival at the depot and our departure was spent perched on a set of stools in the cafeteria. Here we had access to the comings and goings of the travellers courtesy of a large window that surrounded us. While the expresso machine hissed and our beefburgers sizzled on the grill, we took time to let this tapestry unfold before us. It was as if this was the pivotal centre of the county and we watched the masses distribute themselves to their respective areas in order to keep the balance. We played games with their faces and fictionalized fantasies so obviously denied them in real life. We laid wagers of small change on which bus certain individuals might board, and scrutinized every aspect of their person as they sat sipping their coffee and forcing down the yawning edges of an LCT sandwich. Any flaw in someone's character or blemish in their make-up was enough to unleash our sarcasm, as in this idle time they became the butt of our jokes. There is no doubt youth is cruel and a child scars his peers unmercifully. We should have been beyond such actions but unfortunately it was a trait we had not outgrown. Extremely

128

opinionated, we laid waste to the common man, never daring to assess ourselves with such severity lest the chinks in our armour become apparent. Thus we idly passed our time until we clambered aboard the bus and headed back to our territory.

Lincoln was still a metropolis to us, accessible only at such times as this, and it would be a year before we would invade its nightlife. For the present we had to be content as a minor mafia controlling the villages to the west. In this area our world turned slowly as our idle weekends were filled with a routine that kept a consistent orbit of events rotating. Week-nights were normally spent in the Temple Arms drinking and playing snooker while the juke-box cranked out an endless cycle of Jim Reeves records. The same faces filled the same seats and the art of conversation hung limp in a noose above us all.

The Market Slaten dances were few and far between now and, when one did occur, it was a tepid event. Gone were the bristling hordes of greasers locked in their respective packs, their leering looks and glaring antagonism a thing of the past. Where once they lined the walls like assembling tribes, there now languished no more than the odd gaggle of forgotten wallflowers stroking their angoras and patting their hair. Placing their handbags on the dance floor, they swayed round them mechanically to the unchecked feedback blasted forth by some cut-rate local band with powder-blue suits and red Fenders. The freedom we found on the road made more sense to us now, for when we entered these situations we were aware of decay and stagnation. As long as we rose above it and dared to be different there was a chance we might survive.

Hitching and hiking, we still managed to find the occasional place that rated a notch above average. One of these was a large pub called the Green Imp at Wisby Corner. Wisby Corner was little more than a roundabout situated on the A40 between Lincoln and Grantham several miles west of Market Slaten. Sometimes the local sports club from Bramby and Doramby would hold its annual dinner and dance here. These affairs rated high on our social calendar and we would willingly fork out a few quid for a raffle ticket and a chicken dinner. While a hokey band in ill-fitting tuxedos churned out a pot-pourri of current hits, we consumed vast quantities of liquor and twisted the night away. It was a gathering for the young and old alike and the evening's entertainment was sprinkled with polkas and waltzes culminating in a marathon conga line. In our far from sober state, we quite happily attached ourselves to this writhing mass, temporarily relinquishing our grasp on coolness.

It was traditionally a pure northern night, filled with the raucous response of a drunken crowd cheering the finest centre-forwards and fast bowlers in their community. Small silver cups were bestowed on the worthy as jovial emcees saluted them as 'grand lads doing a grand job'. Oh, it was a grand night! We were reasonably well-behaved, but then the fetters had fallen off the whole crowd and even the aged had forgotten decorum and were letting their hair down.

The only incident that caused us any embarrassment was once when Steve, in a particularly paralytic state, decided he wanted to play drums with the band. Not wishing to cause a scene, the drummer relinquished his sticks good-naturedly as Steve, with a satisfied smile, began to thrash unmercifully at the cymbals. Steve's tempo left a lot to be desired, causing the members of the band to turn and stare in his direction, just as he vomited neatly into the snare-drum and fell backwards off the riser on to a passing trolley of custard trifle. Our mortification was beyond expression, and having to carry our puke- and jelly-caked friend across the dance floor and out the front door still haunts me.

Raisin' cain I spit in your eye.

Once a situation occurred when we found ourselves in what appeared to be a dream, only for it to turn out to be a nightmare, bearing in mind that our worst dream was patronization at the hands of the unknown. A small group of seniors existed at Temple Lord who, for want of a better word, might have been referred to as intellectuals; snobs to us, on the lower evolutionary scale. They were elusive and remote from any of the local pubs or functions we frequented, preferring the arty pubs surrounding the cathedral in Lincoln. Automobiles being at their disposal, they were free to travel in the circles they thought bested their image. It was all black turtle necks and white cords, unkempt shoulder-length locks and enough peach fuzz to appear radical. They were not a group we mixed with and we rarely, if ever, came in contact with them. In fact they never crossed our minds,

130

until one night we found ourselves being given a lift by a passing van on its way to a party. The driver and his companions were not at all fazed by our attire and merely picked us up and took us along as if they'd known us for years. After some time, we turned off the main road and began a rough trip down an uneven cowpath leading eventually to a large barn set in a circle of elm trees. The place was dimly lit and clusters of cars were parked in the open area facing the front doors. It was all most intriguing and we fully expected the rip-roaring ding-dong that was normally found at these events. After all, we'd had such experiences at the White Rhino, our own kasbah in the countryside.

On entering there were two things that struck us immediately. One was the lack of light and the other was the music. We were certainly in favour of setting the mood, but it was so dark that all we could make out was a mass of moving shadows. As for the music, it was at the correct volume but was far from being my idea of party sounds. I sure wasn't familiar with it. It resembled moans and groans accompanied by a cat with its tail on fire. On inquiring I was informed that it wasn't a cat but a wolf – a Howlin' Wolf. Thus I was introduced to the blues and Lincolnshire's contemporary underground. I can't say I was impressed at the time; it seemed the entire room was determined to convey misery by intensity, the blues being their own funeral dirge. Loath to enjoy themselves, the guests appeared desperate to assume poses of bohemian intent. Somehow the idea of anarchy in a turnip field didn't quite ring true.

We wandered through the smoky in-crowd like an invisible blot blending in as only we knew how. As our eyes adjusted to the darkness, we could make out close-knit groups of tweed locked in desperate conversation. Our destination was the source of the beer everyone nursed and sipped with little satisfaction. We found it being distributed by a fat brunette standing behind a make-shift bar of hay bales. Like the lead in a Wagnerian opera she loomed over us and demanded our pleasure in a booming basso. Before we had the chance to answer, four cans of luke-warm lager were thrust into our hands. We were all thoroughly sober and totally out of our depth, and it was clear that in order to enjoy our surroundings fully it was necessary to seek out Dutch courage. While Brünnhilde's back was turned, we absconded with a cask of best bitter and a bottle of brandy, found

131

a secluded corner and proceeded to do it as much damage as possible.

Within an hour we were roaring drunk and individually staggering off in search of women of high intelligence and large breasts. Weaving unsteadily through the crowd, I attempted to overhear my friends making contact with various persons in tight sweaters – all except Steve who, to my dismay, was moving through the crowd asking if there was a set of drums around. Eddie had joined an intense discussion and was inquiring if Karl Marx was the one who played the piano or the harp. Rick had dropped his accent, adopting a lilting Irish brogue in an attempt to chat up an emaciated mass of hair and teeth. I left him impressing her with quotations from the Bard, an angle that would soon run out of steam considering Rick's familiarity with poetry and prose began and ended with "Twas on the good ship Venus . . . ' Meanwhile, I sat down on a John Lee Hooker record and attempted to breathe life into my empty bottle.

The next thing I recall is a rough hand shaking my shoulder. The sound of impoverished negroes had been replaced by the distressed bleating of hungry sheep, as I squinted into the face of an old farmhand moving like an angel of mercy through the battlefield. Stumbling through the debris of the night before, he administered his services to the prone corpses littered around the barn. It hadn't been a dream, we had actually been in this den of regional activists who, although knowledgeable about communism in the Third World, had a lot to learn about having a good time. In my drunken stupor, a nightmare had found me fleeing through a cornfield pursued by the operatic Brünnhilde resplendent in Viking helmet and wielding a trident. As my legs lost their momentum, she bore down on me screaming quotations from Chairman Mao, as Howlin' Wolf records rained down on me from all sides. My friends had fared no better. Once their identities had been discovered, they had been ostracized from all conversation and denied access to every inner thigh. Staggering into the daylight, we hot-wired a tractor and made for the main road where we stuck out our thumbs and headed for the Waterloo. A steaming mug of tea and a bacon sarney would be just the thing to erase the memory of a night in the company of Market Slaten's Red Brigade.

Around this time word reached me at school of a job opening in which I might be interested. Summoned back to the office of my pipe-puffing benefactor, I was informed there was a position on the *Lincolnshire Chronicle*. Obviously I was intrigued – here was my chance to cover the local news as 'Scoop Taupin, Ace Reporter'. Fearless in my search for the truth, corruption would crumble under the might of the presses once my pen was unleashed upon the thirsty masses. At night beneath a naked bulb I would hammer out my stories on a hefty typewriter while a diminishing bottle of bourbon stood within arm's reach. My moment of glory was sadly brief. Mr Matlock fired his arrow of reality and my bubble burst, the dream within shattered by the truth. The position was not, as I imagined, in the department of journalism but as a printer's apprentice in the machine room. What was I to do? I had no choice but to accept. If I was to earn a wage at all I would rather do something with prospects as opposed to dead-end labour in the fields. Beaten by the system, I was ordered to report to the management office prior to employment.

I had another month at school before the end of term and my release into the working world. Savour it now, I thought, these weeks are sacred. Nine-to-five routine stared me in the face. This was it, the end of years of questionable education. Responsibility was upon me. To celebrate my entrance into humdrum society the boys and I made plans to check out the action at the Plough. This was one of a number of pubs hiring live bands in order to attract a larger crowd. Far from being the dawn of disco, it was crude entertainment as the club's kitty, being short on cash, only stretched to the minimum in skilled musicians. Still, on a Friday night this new addition to the local scene was a refreshing change and shed a warm light on a cold evening. With Nikki and the boys to raise my spirits, the evening's prospects appeared to be good. There was a lively crowd and an easy atmosphere in the bar, and I imagined it would be a justifiable watering-hole in which to drown my sorrows.

By this time we were big drinkers and, although way below the legal age, ten pints apiece on a Friday night was not unusual. Within an hour we were fired up and ready for the band who were setting up at the end of the room. They were an unimpressive lot with the dull moniker of 'The Undecided'. The guitar player was bearded and intense, the bass player clean-cut

133

and collegiate, while the drummer was indescribable. It wasn't that he was deformed or ugly, he just didn't fit the overall picture. Tall with grubby features, his short dirty blond hair looked as if it might be inhabited. With crumpled shirt and trouser cuffs waving several inches above his ankles, his overall appearance seemed to scream distaste for anything remotely associated with cleanliness. Here before us in all his glorified squalour was the man who within a week would make us mobile, becoming our token friend and taxi-driver.

The boys and I exchanged amused glances and waited for this odd assortment to commence playing. When they did, their music was as uninteresting as they were undecided. Between a succession of twelve-bar blues and badly executed Otis Redding songs, they performed instrumentals of their own design which only accentuated their lack of musical prowess. Making it worse were the bearded guitar player's abortive attempts to bend the strings professionally, an amusing sight and sound which we sarcastically applauded. With the volume at the bar drowning out the volume from their amps, I detected through my deteriorating vision that our abusive heckling, coupled with a lack of enthusiasm from the bar, was having a bad effect on our trio. It was half-way through 'Dimples' that our guitarist came apart at the seams, due quite possibly to our rousing accompaniment, only in our version she had 'pimples in her jaw'. This was the straw that broke the camel's back and, halting the band in mid-song, the guitarist glared in my direction demanding if I could do any better. Any better at this point would mean standing up, something of which I wasn't sure I was capable. It was a stand-off and I'd been called out; high noon at the Plough, with my reputation hanging in the balance. As in all good westerns, the buzz around the bar halted and I could happily have strangled whoever yelled out, 'He couldn't do no warse than you, you big pranny!' Immediately the room exploded with cheers of encouragement. My goose was cooked. If I didn't pull through this I was dead meat. Nikki kissed me with premature pride and Eddie slapped me hard on the back, propelling me unsteadily across the room towards the band.

Fogged by an overabundance of ale, my mind went into overtime, trying desperately to clear the moss that threatened to choke my thought-processes. The bearded one sneered and asked what I was going to sing. With a cocky smile I informed him that after this ordeal I'd be singing hymns at his funeral. Turning to the band I requested Cliff Richard's 'Traveling Light'. It was one of the few songs I knew the words to and I was confident that a bit of Cliff couldn't fail with this crowd. With shrugs of recognition the band struck up as I, with alcoholic courage flowing through my veins, grabbed the mike with professional panache and launched into song. I kept my eyes shut throughout the whole rendition, not wishing to see the reaction of my judge and jury. My sense of melody may have wandered, but I more than made up for it in my passionate delivery, and much to the annoyance of my accompanists I was a resounding success. The crowd was with me from the start and I feel sure several choruses of the telephone directory in Swahili would have guaranteed me the same reaction.

Flushed with pride I made my way through the overflowing glasses of goodwill thrust before me. One of these was purchased by our unusual drummer, who made an effort to introduce himself to me and the boys. He said his name was Neil Gorman and told us he had just recently taken up the drums. Indeed, we thought! He lived in a small cottage on the compound at RAF Woolworth and in the daytime delivered papers from his van. His manner was pleasant but we instinctively judged him to be a crawler – a potentially useful one, but a crawler none the less. Providing we could overcome our distaste for his unsightly pallor, his forest of blackheads and his dandruff, we might possibly utilize his services mercilessly. A van at our disposal could well prove to be useful; we were becoming a little tired of continually having to make our way everywhere on foot. It was just as easy to be revolutionary on four wheels as on two feet. We exchanged numbers and agreed to do something the following weekend. He seemed overjoyed while we remained slightly aloof; after all, we wouldn't have wanted him to think he was immediately accepted by us.

By the time last orders were called I was legless and charging around the parking lot in pursuit of Nikki. It had begun to rain and my idiotic war whoops bounced off the walls in the hollow night. Suddenly Nikki was gone along with most of the cars. I turned and saw headlights entering the forecourt at the far end of the pub, and in my temporary insanity imagined it was Nikki being transported off by someone else. Hollering at the top of my lungs, I lurched like a mad dripping hunchback towards the approaching vehicle and, as it pulled up before me, staggered defiantly into the brilliance of the headlights. Steaming like a cart horse, I slammed my fist into the bonnet and roared, 'Where's my bird, you bastard?' The driver's door opened and out stepped my father. He was not pleased. 'The boys called,' he said. 'They thought you might need a lift home.' I sank to my knees clasping my head in my hands, rain-soaked and wretched.

Things never got too bad at home but I can't say my father was overjoyed at my antics. I spent little time helping out around the farm and kept irregular hours for someone still at school. To top it all, I'd got into the habit of filching the odd fiver from his wallet. While everything else I got up to didn't worry me one iota, this petty thievery of my father's hard-earned cash preyed on my mind. I made promises to myself that some day I would repay him in full, but nothing could alleviate the guilt I felt at robbing from my own family. What made things worse was the fact that no matter how erratic I became in my behaviour, there always remained a stability in our household that made me feel at one with it. My parents were pleased I'd found a job with prospects and imagined responsibility would keep me in check once I began life as a working man. However, that was not to be, and I was to run them through a gauntlet of ups and downs before setting things right.

I turned sixteen in May of 1966 as the Beatles released 'Paperback Writer' and the Stones delivered 'Paint it Black'. Across the sea, the magic of Brian Wilson was at its zenith as the Beach Boys' harmonies enveloped us all with 'God Only Knows'. Dylan's music was exceptionally abstract at this time with songs such as 'Can You Please Crawl Out of Your Window' and 'Rainy Day Women Nos 12 and 35'. He continued to alienate many die-hard folk fans who resented the fact that he had plugged in and gone electric at the Newport Jazz Festival. School was winding down for the summer holidays and preparing for the exodus. Now that the comfort of my educational cocoon was drawing to a close, I became increasingly aware that soon I would be fending for myself in an unmerciful world. I'd never been too keen on school, but for the most part it had been a crystal-clear excuse against the rigours of wage-earning. My stay of execution had come to an end and no reprieve was in sight. The boot had been administered and, about to walk the plank, I prayed that the waters would be clear of sharks.

The final week was a series of anti-climactic goodbyes for, aside from Danny, there were really very few of my classmates and teachers whom I was not happy to see the back of. As for the girls in my class including Priscilla, Daphne and the blossoming twins, I would no doubt continue to see them here and there. The rest could crawl into their tractor cabs and disappear up their own furrows for all I cared. When the last day arrived I treated it as the end of another week and, without glancing back, walked out of those gates for ever. The faces of those with whom I'd shared lessons disappeared like puffs of smoke never to be seen again. Sad to say I felt no regret – honesty is a cruel executioner.

. . . I only farmed in schools that were so worn and torn.

In the months leading up to my departure from the secondary system the boys and I had been making good use of our new toady. The derelict drummer from the Plough had gone all out catering to our every whim, picking us up at our beck and call and dropping us off late at night. Although our feet were called on occasionally to get us around, it was in Neil Gorman's old blue van that we majestically conquered the countryside. There were no back seats so we sprawled horizontally on the floor in the rear, taking turns to ride shotgun up front. The amount of junk that littered this vehicle was amazing. Anything Neil thought might be of the slightest use was hurled in and hooked up, the most remarkable being a record player. It was somehow connected to the battery and sat jammed between the front seats, compensating for his non-existent radio. The drawbacks to this insane sound system were obvious, and we seldom got to hear the complete cycle of any forty-five, with the needle skipping over the discs as the van bumped and lurched down highway and byway.

Neil's house was an extension of his van. Untidy and dirty, it came complete with an archaic mother who remained in her room for the entire time we associated with him. Occasionally when Neil took her in a cup of tea we would catch a glimpse of her sitting motionless in an upright chair, draped in a shawl and facing the wall. We were of the opinion she was quite dead and that Neil, having never said two words to her, was unaware of the fact. It didn't seem to bother him one way or the other, as he merely regarded her as part of the furnishings.

Neil rose early each morning to deliver his papers and it was with regard to this occupation that he had sucked up to us in the first place. He had a rival in the delivery business who was becoming more successful by snatching many of Neil's orders from under his nose. Basically gutless, Neil had decided that, rather than use his non-existent charm to win back his clients, he'd hire some unscrupulous persons to sabotage the competition. He delicately approached us with this proposition, not wishing to offend us by inferring that we were the slightest bit dishonest, but at the same time aware that rumour had it that we would do anything for the right price.

Later that night we set out to do the dirty dead. Equipped with two pounds of sugar and decked out in full commando attire, we pulled up outside the home of our friend's adversary. Like Neil's dwelling, it was remote. Presumably those who rise early to deliver papers in all kinds of weather need the solitude befitting madmen. The situation was to our advantage, as the caravan in which he lived was a comfortable distance from the battered Cortina in which he made his rounds. Our plan was simple: unscrew his petrol cap, pour in the sugar and wham! – out of commission. Without his motor he would be unable to do his job and his annoyed customers would turn to another for delivery of their dailies.

From inside the caravan an oil lamp flickered as the sound of radio static crackled, causing a buzz of intensity to fill the evening air. The smell of the night was heavy on the dense patches of nettles and fern, and clouds of gnats rose from pools of stagnant oil and water reflected against the moon. Our target was a collector of junk and, as we moved in closer, all manner of rusting machinery materialized before our eyes. In the half-light, indistinguishable articles appeared before us like Trojan sentries wrapped in iron, peering down on us with accusation in their eyes. We felt a sense of urgency in the air, the unshakeable feeling one gets when being watched by unseen eyes. We would have abandoned the vicinity in panic had we not been so close to completing our mission. Quickly I unscrewed the petrol cap as Rick and Steve hoisted the damaging substance. The moment the sugar began its flow of destruction we heard the ghostly sound of unravelling chain. Our blood froze and the bag split as Rick and Steve dived in different directions.

A howl broke the night air as we turned to face the oncoming charge of a large black dog bearing a set of unpleasant teeth. Manacled like some berserk slave, it tore towards us, its green satanic eyes spelling destruction. With a victorious roar it hurled itself into the air and, just when I thought my life was dogmeat, it boomeranged back from whence it came with a strangled whine. Luckily for me it had reached the end of its tether and lay panting in frustration somewhere in the darkness. Breathing sighs of relief we immediately set about concluding our business, as the aggravated hound regarded us with a defeated look. As we were finishing we heard the sound of yet another dog in the distance. This was a hysterical high-pitched yapping, not the slightest bit intimidating, coming from beyond the trees away from where we were working. Still, all the noise it was making was bound to attract attention and, quickly cleaning up our mess, we moved stealthily back towards Neil's van.

Just as we reached the road we turned to see the other dog tearing towards us as fast as its tiny legs could propel it. This time we made no move to run and stood laughing as the minute white poodle careered towards us. How strange to secure a bona-fide guard dog and let this little runt run loose scaring no one! At least that's what we thought, until the miniature menace scrambled up the back of Rick's trouser leg and attached itself to his bum. With a shriek of horror, Rick galloped off down the road with this canine limpet swinging left and right like a snowy tail on our friend's rear end. Recovering from our hysterics and with our mission now accomplished, we set out for home. Needless to say, Rick didn't ride shotgun but lay face down in the back, silent and unamused.

Immediately following this incident we enlisted Neil's help in another exercise in law-breaking. This one was to leave us with an over-abundance of certain articles and a large amount of egg on our faces. There was a popular transport café on the road between Market Slaten and Woolworth which catered to lorry drivers and local labourers. It was the genuine article, small, smelly and cramped with grease-stained windows and sugar spoons chained to the table. The tea was served in pint mugs and the menu changed frequently, serving satisfying grub designed to fill out the ample waistlines of ravenous road-rats. During the day it did a roaring trade but in the evening it tended to be fairly quiet, and it was then that we decided to strike. Our objective was to rip off the condom machine in the toilet, figuring that truckers, being the randy sods they are, must invest a tidy sum in Durex. Neil stayed in the car with the engine running while Rick remained outside the loo keeping an eye open for anyone on their way in. Meanwhile Eddie, Steve and I ran in with a couple of crowbars, ripped the machine off the wall and made off into the night. This lightning raid went according to plan and, before we knew it, we were back in the van fleeing to safety.

Once we reached a spot that was safe and quiet we piled out and proceeded to prise open our acquisition. It was not as easy as expected and took some time before the oblong box exploded under pressure, showering a spray of nuts and bolts in all directions. What little coinage there was within went the same way, landing in a slime-ridden ditch to the right of us. Not feeling there was enough drowned silver to send us scrambling beneath the poisoned waters, we turned our attention to doling out the rubbers, of which there were countless dozens. Obviously our opinion on the sex life of the long-distance lorry driver was a myth or they preferred to let their women take the precautions. As I sifted through the condoms doing 'one for you and one for me', I came across a key which, without thinking, I hurled into the ditch. As the plop of the key died in my ears, my arm froze and my heart sank. We looked at each other in disbelief as in unison we realized what I had done. In my impatience to deal a fair round of condoms, I had cast away the spare key, one that could have unlocked a multitude of similar machines. Instantaneously we dived towards the sight of the dying ripple. Slipping and sliding down the bank we sloshed into the water undeterred by the filth around us. We must have searched for an hour or so until we were caked from head to toe. It was to no avail, the key was gone for ever, hidden from our thieving hands by a just God. We emerged from the ditch like a tribe of repellent humanoids from the deep. What had begun as the perfect crime had spiralled into disaster, leaving us penniless but well protected!

We made full use of our haul, testing their capacity for water, inflating them and sending them skyward, even painting them in assorted colours and tying them to the local bobby's Vespa. Not one, however, was used for the very reason they were manufactured in the first place. We were still confirmed virgins with big mouths and the crudest of induction into slap and tickle. While I still languished in the delights that were Nikki, Rick had taken up with a pleasant girl from Market Slaten called Connie. Connie was extremely demure, very shy and not one for the indecent sorties we made into the night. Occasionally this tended to split us up and, while Rick held hands with his new love on the sofa of her parents' humble home, we carried on in normal fashion. My relationship with Nikki was loose and getting looser, and while Rick relished his own form of trainee matrimony, I preferred to run wild. Steve dabbled in the occasional affair, brief encounters tending to fizzle out before they began. Eddie seemed incapable of remaining interested in any one female for more than an evening, a tendency of which I was jealous but was unable to emulate. I wanted to stash my own property away and bring it out when I needed attention. Naturally Nikki's independence wasn't going to buy this situation, and by the time school was out, so was Nik.

Steve had begun working a year earlier at a dairy in Lincoln, Rick was preparing for agricultural college and Eddie was still commuting to school in Grimsby. There was no way to hold back time and the responsibility of employment loomed like a dark cloud on the horizon. I didn't feel any different. Was I supposed to, or was it just a minor step and gradual change that would descend on me, turning me from irresponsible wastrel into model citizen? I seriously doubted it. We still stared conformity in the face with our tongues firmly in our cheeks. I saw only a vision of continued contamination of public decency at the hands of our decadent youth.

Ten

It had come to this – after years of daydreaming in the confines of my own mind, I had become what I vowed I would never be, a cog in the endless wheel. True, I was not labouring on the land tilling the soil and bringing in the sheaves, but as I arrived at work on my first day the thought of stubble and soil didn't seem half as bad as they once had.

Rising several hours earlier with the grey dawn breaking over my sleepy village, I had been loath to leave my warm bed. A savage rainfall driven by a howling north-east wind was beating against the windows as I dragged my tired body down the freezing corridor to the bathroom. Nothing could be more depressing. The hour was ungodly and only the smell of breakfast prevented me from kicking my younger brother out of bed in spite. How lucky he was to be still warm beneath the sheets, coddled in the comfort of primary school. My parents did their best to make the time of day seem normal. My father had already been up and out feeding the chickens and my mother had packed my lunch and been cooking breakfast for the last hour. How I envied their strength! What did I have to complain about? After all, here I was lucky to be employed and have a family considerate enough to be aware of my reservations. If this was the way it was to be, then it was up to me to make the best of it. 'Grow up,' I told myself, 'come to terms with life and think yourself lucky.' I still felt depressed.

With my collar turned up and my rucksack over my shoulder, I stepped into the grim morning. It had been arranged that our next-door neighbour who worked in Lincoln would give me a ride into town each day, and in return for a little greasing of the palm I was duly deposited outside the offices of the Lincolnshire Standard Group. Doing my best to alleviate my blue funk, I made my way as instructed to the management office, where I received a cold and formal reception from a man neither charming nor comforting. After a ten-minute dissertation on work procedure, he sent for Len the foreman, under whose wing I was expected to learn the trade. Len appeared in brown overalls covered in printer's ink, fawned beautifully in the presence of his superior and led me off. He wasn't completely disagreeable but did seem to have a decidedly *Daily Mirror* mentality and, once I got to know him better, I was of the opinion he most definitely slept at night under the red flag. Still, there were times when a ray of humanity shone through and in the coming weeks he did make a reasonable effort to educate me in his trade.

The machine room where I worked was long and high with dirty skylights in the roof allowing in the minimum of daily sunshine. The room was illuminated by three oblong fixtures giving off a sickly neon glow, and coupled with the ever-present thunder of machinery this caused constant headaches. The place was a Dickensian nightmare where no one seemed able to afford a smile and greetings were grudgingly bestowed. My co-workers varied from dull and dreary to plain obnoxious, including two exceptionally plebeian Jack-the-lad types who insisted on playing 'Let's make a monkey out of the new boy'. I went along with these inane initiations and dutifully went off in search of straight S-hooks and glass hammers. My initial wage was six pounds a week, normal pay for any trainee apprentice. It was also expected that I enroll in night school in order to qualify for my diploma when I reached twenty-one. Twenty-one! God, that was five years away, and it suddenly became apparent that this labour was expected of me for ever. Before my eyes appeared nightmarish images of treading in ever-diminishing circles like some mutant worker from Fritz Lang's *Metropolis*.

The machine room contained two large presses that dealt with commercial work such as catalogues and posters, while I was assigned to one of two small Heidelbergs used for lesser jobs such as business cards and tickets. The operation of these machines was relatively simple and within a few days I had mastered it without much trouble. So here I was in the belly of the British work force, one more card on the clock, and as I left for home after my first day I couldn't help but feel destiny had dealt me a cruel blow.

To celebrate my first day in the den of the red I thought it appropriate to call up the boys and descend on several boozers. Naturally Neil transported us, and as we embarked on a marathon pub crawl, I related in detail the ups and downs of my new career. Now that we were thoroughly mobile there were no limitations on the public houses we might frequent. The Temple still remained our stronghold, and in the weeks that followed we met another amiable lad who would lend himself to us as a means of transportation.

Shannon Wheeler was one of the most instantly likeable chaps we'd ever encountered. In his early twenties, he had an irresistible twinkle in his eyes that assured us he would never be dull company. Shannon's brother Tommy also became friendly with us in time. He was the area's most notorious Cassanova and between the two of them they generated a fair amount of charisma. Shannon enjoyed our company and together we spent many riotous nights in the pursuit of sustenance and passion. However, I learned early on that keeping up with Shannon was not as easy as it seemed.

Around this time there was a party at the home of a certain Ron Evans. Ron was pleasant but rather dull, and had organized a bash to concur with his parents' absence from town. A dangerous endeavour, considering he'd invited half the town, half of which respected property the way Attila respected Rome. On the night of the party I made a concerted effort to tog up in my best gear, which included a turtle-neck insert. This was a turtle-neck with front and back flap which you wore under your shirt like a tucked-in bib. They were rather smart and the overall effect left me feeling like an up-market vicar.

We decided to make an early start of it and were in the pub at opening time throwing back double vodkas with alarming regularity. From this point the evening became a blur, and in no time at all Shannon and I had become separated from the rest of the group. We remained caught up in a marathon drinking session with a long-lost friend of Shannon's. As much as I admired my capacity at the time, it was non-existent compared to these old hands. The mix of drinks shifted with each round. One minute we were gulping Guinness and whisky chasers, the next it

144

was brandy or gin. Diligently I stuck with them, my foolish pride leading me down a path to destruction. By this time I was incapable of speech and without the solid back of a good chair would have been crawling round the floor. Suddenly Shannon remembered the party and steered me out into the cold night air, which had a sobering effect enabling me to stumble to my companion's car. I don't remember the festivities and only recall crashing through the front door into the crowd assembled in the entrance. The remainder of this incident is based on the story recounted to me days later by my bemused friends.

According to them I continued to drink anything and everything in sight, including wine, port and several foreign liqueurs. At one point I was even found in the kitchen knocking back Mrs Evans's cooking sherry. Several hours hence I was nowhere to be found and an immediate search party was formed to locate me. Ten minutes later I was discovered in a field at the back of the house brandishing a bottle of Crème de Menthe before a herd of terrified cows. My objective was to share this liqueur with the startled Friesians in order to obtain green milk, and I became rather belligerent when requested to cease my experiment. Most of my rescuers were in favour of violence to quieten my tantrum, while those close to me argued for a stay of execution and led me away puking all over their shoes. My puking in fact became ceaseless and soon I was a complete mess, to the point where I was untouchable. The only solution was to strip me down and bundle me into the back of Shannon's car. This was achieved with much revulsion on the part of the boys, who in my eyes won their true colours that night for pure devotion to a worthless cause.

Obviously it was not wise to let my parents see me in this state and they decided to store my catatonic carcass at a friend's house. Duly achieved, straws were drawn to see who would inform my parents that, due to circumstances beyond anyone's control, their son would be spending the night elsewhere. I awoke the next morning on the top level of a bunk bed and immediately thought I'd been shanghaied. The room swayed and my head ached as I rolled over and crashed to the floor where I lay naked and nauseous. Clinging to the bedpost for support, I attempted to rise from a foetal position only to catch my reflection in a full-length mirror across the room. I was appalled! Staring back at me was Death, green and stooped, its hair in shock, dung-caked and with a rancid scalp. Below this terrifying mop, crimson pinpoints stared vacantly like dead pools in a field of swollen flesh. All that remained of the human element was a turtle-neck bib, virginal white against my septic nakedness.

The reception I got when I made it home was one of total excommunication. With his usual knack for punishment by silence, my father looked through me as if I were worthless air. Even my mother, who was sympathetic under normal circumstances, was surprisingly frosty. It was a week before this icy environment thawed and things got back to normal. For those seven long days the punishment of alienation was enough to make me swear to change my ways. If only it could have been that simple.

The summer of '66 was at its height and for the boys and me the months between August and November rang in many changes. With the exception of Eddie we'd all left school and were gainfully employed, and with new friends like Neil and Shannon it was possible for us to spread our influence farther afield. No longer having to travel afoot, we abandoned our fatigues and parkas and took to dressing in a more conservative style. Being totally erratic and contradictory, slipping into conformity came easily.

Beyond the boundaries of our shallow world the Sixties were shaping up for a cultural revolution that was to make it the most charismatic decade in history. Across the sea in Vietnam, a senseless war was claiming the lives of countless thousands incapable of comprehending the hell in which they fought and died. In Alabama years of racial hatred exploded in the streets as the heat of the southern sun turned Selma into a pressure-cooker. In space the New Frontier was experiencing an invasion from earth, as the superpowers hurled billions of dollars worth of scientific machinery into orbit. The world, it seemed, had gone insane. In the streets there were demonstrations and riots, art had become avant-garde, skirts had gone within inches of decency and Twiggy and the Shrimp ruled the runways of fashion. All this had little effect on us as we toasted our bums before the fire in the Temple lounge.

I was far more concerned with the fit of my new suit, a sharp blue number I had purchased at great expense and with considerable pride from Burton's in Lincoln. I stood there

146

cradling my pint like some regional spiv, the problems of the world remaining the oblique headlines of yesterday's paper. If we were indeed on the doorstep of more turbulence to come, so be it, for the boys and I were building walls in our ears and becoming complacent. Perhaps the archaic ideology of our local peers was not so bad, and remaining ignorant of current events could have its advantages. I was feeling decidedly more comfortable with these older carefree wide-boys who drank, gambled and walked through life at their own pace. What the hell! I was having a good time and it wasn't my job to change the world. Everything was a million miles away; here I was king of the hill and it felt good. My dreams were lethargic and lay dormant, and it seemed the butterfly had at last been broken on the wheel.

Life was becoming an endless chain of work and play. During the week I dutifully went to the former with little enthusiasm, returning on Friday nights with a meagre wage, intent on raising hell. My father had given up hope that his sons might continue in his footsteps and the farm had long since been sold. He had become a civil servant certifying cattle for the Ministry of Agriculture, a ball-busting job that took its toll. From the time he started, the beasts he fought to sort through began to bruise and batter him. He constantly returned home with some new wound, hobbling across the lawn in the seeping damp of winter, valiantly making light of his latest cuts and bruises. This was not the legacy he deserved and it was apparent that the English winter was not his friend.

Strictly from the old school
he was quiet about his pain.

Most weekends were repetitious affairs. Toffed up in our suits and reeking of Old Spice we disappeared into the night to make the usual rounds of pubs and country clubs, the latter being an attempt to educate the rural *nouveau riche* to a more cosmopolitan nightlife. They were in fact glorified boozers, glossed over with cheap pretentious trappings, intimidating the locals into feeling it was necessary to hold your pint by the handle. Usually policed by swarthy employees with fake Italian accents in ratty-looking tuxedos, they treated the customers with contempt. Clad in this evening attire, the bouncers looked even more ridiculous than usual and stood around like enormous penguins, their flabby guts held in by beer-stained cummerbunds.

Taking a date to one of these places was a seal of serious intent. It wasn't cheap for anyone as hard up as we were, and with the optional steak supper, things got pretty pricey before the night was out. A few vodka and limes along with your own ale consumption could send the old wallet into a state of shock. Unless there was the definite possibility of a good grope later in the evening, we came unaccompanied. Your best bet was to hit the unattached at the end of the night, half an hour before closing time. This way it was two drinks at the most and a good chance the evening's intake had turned your prey into a raving nympho.

Other places we hit occasionally were the Boston Gliderdrome and the Mecca Ballroom in Grimsby, where top-line performers and bands could be seen live. This was indeed the big time, and although out of our tribal jurisdiction, we were always guaranteed a night to remember. The Gliderdrome with its ballroom lit up like the night sky with a thousand coloured Christmas lights was our favourite. An enormous mirrored ball rotated in the centre with hypnotic frequency, emitting dazzling pinspots of light on the crowd below. The bar was a work of art – 200 yards in length, it wound round the room like an alcoholic stairway to heaven, but for all its enormity buying a drink was a battle in itself. It was normally the dance-oriented bands that dominated the billing, and groups such as Geno Washington's Ram Jam Band and Jimmy James and the Vagabonds were particular favourites who were featured frequently. However, it was the appearance of Otis Redding, the American soul legend, that paled all I had seen before. I was a fan anyway, but never expected to be affected the way I was that Saturday night in the autumn of '66. While the crowd around me pushed and shoved and sweated, nothing detracted from the man on stage. For an instant in this year of my own ignorance I felt dwarfed by the voice and sheer presence of this man. To me there had always been magic in music, but never until this moment had I seen it powered by such electricity. I realized then that music was possibly the greatest politician in the world and the stage the ultimate platform of communication.

Grimsby tended to be a little more hairy than Boston, and the crowd attending the Mecca seemed slightly more aggressive. It was necessary at times to remain in a group to maintain a show of strength, which we managed to do with Shannon rounding out the numbers. Neil, on the other hand, proved to be useless and fled to the Gents at the slightest hint of altercation. The only time we had any trouble was when Eddie, returning in a separate car, stopped off at the chip shop for a snack. Being Eddie, he retaliated when a drunken docker dipped into his bag of chips for a free meal. Had it only been the two of them, Eddie might have stood a chance. Unfortunately this was not the case, and our pal was the object of much thumping as he became a punch-bag for a bunch of thugs. We decided to form a posse and take revenge, but to our good fortune we never discovered the culprits. The more we considered our adversaries, the less confident we became, finally realizing that discretion was the better part of valour.

If it wasn't the chip shop on the way home then it was a swift meal at the Chinky, depending on how affluent we felt that week. Back then a Number Three upstairs at the Foo Yung, complete with flock wallpaper and formica tables, was akin to Friday night at Maxim's. I hate to think what went into the dishes coming out of the kitchen disguised as egg rolls and sweet and sour. The non-committal look of our waiter was giving nothing away and the drunken clientele was far too pissed to presume this was anything but the real thing. Boy, this was living – true adult behaviour! Clubs, restaurants – what else could there possibly be?

After a good night I was dropped back home and would find my mother still up reading or doing *The Times* crossword. It was a warm feeling to find her there and we would sit together for a short time and talk. Her gentle manner had a sobering effect and helped recharge my batteries lest the engine of my enthusiasm for life die completely. After she kissed my cheek and went to bed, I normally stumbled around the kitchen creating a sandwich of major proportions. Carving doorstep slices from a farmhouse loaf, I would insert between them anything edible residing in the fridge, washing it all down with several pints of gold top. After this unsettling snack I retired, thinking perhaps it was true what they said about Chinese food.

During the late autumn the boys and I were offered an irresistible bargain. Digger Thomas, the overdressed heavy from the Bealby Youth Club incident, had decided to part with his motorcycle. The asking price was ten pounds, a sum we could just about afford if we pooled our resources. The idea of owning our own bike on which to do a spot of scrambling was tempting and we decided to make the investment. We met one Saturday afternoon in the Temple car park to exchange money for machine. Being a little schizophrenic, Digger was not the sort to haggle with, so we thought it best not to quibble about the price. After an unconvincing run-down of the bike's capabilities, Digger pocketed his tenner and took off. His exit was rather hasty and we were immediately struck by the feeling we'd been conned. I didn't like to think we'd been cheated by a lower life form, but on closer inspection of this rusting heap it was hard not to come to this conclusion.

As Steve was the oldest, he was nominated to ride the bike to Eddie's, and after a good push he disappeared up the road in a cloud of blue smoke. With Steve dispatched on to the highway, we got on our bicycles and rode home, presuming we would find him waiting for us on our arrival. Several hours later he had still not turned up and it was getting close to nightfall when a Land Rover towing a horse box roared into the yard. It skidded to a halt beside us and a good-natured young man jumped out, beckoning us to the rear of the trailer. 'I think this belongs to you,' he said with a laugh, unfastening the dead-bolts and dropping the tailboard. Fast asleep amid a pile of rancid hay lay Steve surrounded by an assortment of motorcycle parts, a sight that did not meet with our approval. Although we were grateful for the return of our mate, we were not happy to see our purchase in pieces. It was a sheepish Steve East who recounted his trip home, a journey fraught with danger from the moment the cycle hit the road.

No sooner had he reached the outskirts of Market Slaten than the bike died and Steve glided to a halt. Checking the tank he found the petrol level to be fine and set about restarting the bike, which he managed to do, only to have it conk out again a hundred yards farther on. It stubbornly refused to start again and our friend was forced to push it homewards. Soon a sympathetic old couple in a Morris Minor took pity on Steve's sad plight, tying a rope to the handlebars with the intention of towing him home. All went well for several miles until, just as Steve was beginning to feel comfortable, the front wheel disconnected itself, rolling into a nearby field. This left Steve airborne while the rest of our acquisition hurtled down the road behind the vanishing Morris.

Suffering only a few minor cuts and bruises Steve set off with the wheel under his arm, intent on relocating the remainder of the machine. He found it strewn about and steaming several miles ahead. Unaware that Steve had come adrift, his rescuers continued happily dragging the remains of our bike until it worked itself loose. By now Steve was at his wits' end. Here he was, miles from home, with a front wheel under his arm and a heap of junk at his feet. It was while pondering this situation that he was rescued by our friend with the horse box. All that remained now was to attempt some form of wizardry to re-form our wrecked motorbike to its original state, an operation taking all the ingenuity we could muster. With the help of a mechanically-minded farmhand, we managed to resurrect it to a shadow of its former self. For a few weeks it gave us several enjoyable rides before it packed up permanently and was sold to the local scrapman for ten bob.

The decline in vehicles at our command was reaching epidemic proportions. First our bike had gone and now Neil was having trouble keeping his decaying heap intact. Even Shannon, whose car was an impeccable monolith of engineering, was about to meet with bad luck. Returning home from a late-night date, he'd been fiddling with the radio when his car hit an oil slick on a narrow country lane. All he remembered of the incident was his car sailing through the air as Bobby Darin sang 'If I Were a Carpenter'. This was a stroke of misfortune all round, and although we could still count on Neil occasionally, it was Shannon's car we particularly missed. Neil was becoming more irritable and tending to complain about the cost of petrol. His morose attitude was annoying, and if at all possible we tried to make other arrangements in order not to be dependent on him.

We sympathized with Shannon entirely and stuck by him in his hour of need, including him in all of our alternative plans. Together the five of us would go on major pub crawls or attend the weekend dances in Shelton. Many evenings would find us sitting in the Temple Arms cracking jokes and making plans for club night. Club night was something the publican had started, to thank his younger patrons who had made the Temple as popular as it was. The room where it was held was small and cramped due to the numbers attending. At the same time, though, it was warm and friendly with a regular crowd that could be counted on to get along and cause no trouble. The music was good, thanks to an older lad called Bill Brown who acted as the club's unofficial host. He was a serious bloke with a pleasant enough attitude and a great record collection. It was his discs that were played, and although no one was allowed near them, I was most impressed with his choices. Here in these relaxed surroundings Shannon, the boys and I managed to forget the drudgery of the working day and laugh about life without its bitter twists and pitfalls getting the better of us.

Monday brought the routine week back and I set off again into a world of overalls and ink. By now I had spent several months on the job and things hadn't improved. In fact I was more depressed and disinterested than ever, an attitude Len was obviously picking up on. I got the impression he already had me earmarked as a malcontent, and the way I reluctantly gave up my weekly donation to the odious little weasel from the union did not go unnoticed. I was not being subversive, I just found the whole ideology of 'yes, brother, no, brother' antiquated and distasteful. Nothing I did could shake the feeling that I was caught up in some cold northern regime. More than once Len pulled me into casual conversation only to end up quizzing me on my recreational interests, which I perceived as an attempt to check out whether my outside activities were radical enough to substantiate his suspicions. Once he approached me as I was printing up tickets for a local rock festival, inquiring whether I was at all interested in pop music. His words were spat out with such contempt that, not wishing to make waves, I denied the one interest that really made me happy. This refusal to acknowledge my true passion depressed me, making me feel like Peter denying Christ. That lunch hour I walked up Lindum Hill and into the gardens of the Museum of Modern Art, sat down on the grass and contemplated my sad state of affairs. Fumes from the trucks rumbling up the hill and grinding their gears floated in on the air, making my head throb, and the incessant chatter of nearby office workers and shop girls irritated me and made my heart ache. Everywhere I turned I saw no pity and no compromise to the situation. Above the haze of industrial exhaust that clouded my thoughts, the sun still shone and the sky remained a brilliant blue, but none of it held any comfort. There was nothing for it; if I was to remain sane I had to find alternative employment. I didn't want to be a hero or shake any literary pillars, all I wanted was fresh air and freedom to move. This factory with its claustrophobic socialism was killing me.

> *Razor blades and common trade*
> *Throats cut on the working man.*

I'd a tendency to hero-worship certain individuals not really worthy of such devotion. Several would come later on, but one I felt drawn to at this time was a moody eighteen-year-old called Tim Green. Tim had few friends and ran with no pack, and in my opinion was the local James Dean. His demeanour was one of attractive aloofness, making me all the more interested. On weekends Tim scrambled bikes at the Stone Pit, and the boys and I often went to watch him race his stripped-down Dot across the rough terrain. During the week he was employed by a local juke-box and fruit-machine dealer called Syd Summers. Tim, with his partner Tony, travelled the countryside fixing any of Syd's machines that were on the blink. It was this aspect of his life that most appealed to me, and the idea of spending time tinkering with these recreational toys in pubs and clubs around the area held a distinct romantic fascination. Tim was only a nodding acquaintance and spent most of his weekends drinking in Lincoln, zipping back and forth in a souped-up Mini Cooper. It was one of those eye-catchers that had been altered mechanically to sound like an MX missile, and it could frequently be seen barrelling by in a cloud of dust, all aerials and headlights. It was to this pinnacle of wreckless bravado that I now attempted to climb.

Nikki was friendly with Syd Summers and his crew and had promised to check out any job openings. Unfortunately this caused me to become over-confident and jump the gun, and with premature thoughts of being one of Syd's colourful troubleshooters my work in the printing room dropped to a slovenly crawl. I had no time for racks and rollers, my mind full of a future in the gypsy task-force chatting up barmaids and knocking back free pints as I emptied fruit machines with Tim. My unproductive attitude caused Len to come down heavily on me until my temper, normally kept in check, snapped. Confident that my prospects of a job with Syd were in the bag, I turned on Len, drowning him in a tirade of verbal abuse. The outcome, of course, was dismissal. Determined not to leave without some show of distaste for the operation that had made my life miserable, I turned and flung my ink trowel into the guts of my loathsome Heidelberg, causing the machine to malfunction and grind to a halt. Len turned scarlet, swearing my life would lead me to the gallows, and screamed that I had thrown away a career that could mean security for me in years to come. No good was to come of me! I was destined to spend my life living on the dole until I was left slugging meths in a back alley. That was it! I'd literally thrown the spanner in the works and become unemployed for the first time in my life.

I assured my distressed parents it was only temporary and that my job with Syd would be materializing any day. Not totally convinced, they found it hard to see a future in servicing fruit machines, but retained a positive attitude and, with their usual non-dramatic stance, stood back to see what tomorrow might bring. In this case tomorrow brought Christmas Eve, an occasion which under any other circumstances would have been a happy event. Unfortunately it brought the news that not only had Syd no place for me in his organization, but he was also extremely annoyed I'd even had the nerve to feel I'd been considered. I was devastated; in fact I felt so low I even turned down an offer from Tim who, at Nikki's request, called to invite me to a Christmas Eve party in Lincoln. My heart wouldn't have been in it and ultimately this turned out to be the smartest move of my life. Waking on Christmas morning I learned that Tim's Mini had been cut in two by an articulated lorry. Tim had been killed instantly.

Eleven

The pain of living in an adult world had become excruciating and as the New Year began I felt my life was in ruins. Nothing seemed to matter any more as I wandered aimlessly into 1967 unemployed and angry. I was aware of my failures and, if indeed this was my penance for presuming too much, then it was harsh retribution. The sentence life was handing me could not have been worse, and I walked around alone with a chip on my shoulder and a ball and chain dragging me down. During the week I cycled into Market Slaten and spent hours in the Temple bar nursing a drink, staring listlessly into the amber liquid. When the pub shut I moved around the corner to the Waterloo and sat alone drinking endless cups of tea and playing the juke-box. Walking the streets only made things worse, for I would see my friends working in the shops along the main street. Occasionally they would come out and chat and I would make light of my situation so as not to appear bitter. They knew me as a fun character who took life with a pinch of salt, and I was not about to let them see me looking morose and lost in the wilderness.

At home I stared at the television for hours without any of it sinking in, my concerned parents looking on but saying nothing. The only thing that ignited a spark of interest was seeing Jimi Hendrix for the first time. His appearance on 'Top of the Pops' in January was sensational. Suddenly out of nowhere came this skinny black ragdoll possessed of electricity and fired by an intensity that turned his guitar into an extension of his body. In three short minutes he managed to put his instrument through a series of gymnastics that transgressed the borders of conventional style. I knew things were getting pretty outrageous in the rock world, but this incantation transcended anything that had come before. Once again the power of pop was motivating me. Its healing agents worked wonders on my depleted system and sent shock-waves to my tired brain. As if this wasn't enough, the Beatles had just followed their classic 'Strawberry Fields Forever' with the even more astounding 'Sergeant Pepper's Lonely Hearts Club Band'. I was both mesmerized and frustrated. Out there beyond the barriers that confined me to my roots was a vibrant world of sight and sound. All I could do was sit for hours listening to my treasured discs, dreaming I was somehow a part of it all. What hope had I? At the rate I was going I wouldn't even be able to afford to keep abreast of the rock world I cherished.

I missed my friends terribly during the week, and moving around without them was a strange feeling. I was without doubt the angry young man, lost and confused with rock and roll as my saving grace. Out of frustration and boredom I started hanging around with a selection of characters with whom I shared the common bond of redundancy. I spent most of my time with a lad called Mark Haynes who was twenty-three and looked about forty. Mark had been educated at Temple Lord and had been a star pupil; he was bright and absolutely despised being so. He had held several accountancy jobs and been dismissed from most of them, his lack of enthusiasm going unappreciated. In fact, he had been fired from his last position for supposedly fiddling the books and was still in the process of being investigated. Mark was tall and had once been reasonably good-looking. Not one to care about his appearance, he had let himself go and his face had become puffy due to drink. His curly hair had thinned and was turning prematurely grey. Through Mark I began to fall back into my old attitude of accepting the inevitable and was soon living the life of Riley at the expense of my father's good nature. Why my father supported me in these lost months was hard to fathom. I can only suppose he still believed that somewhere down the line I might find what I was ultimately looking for. At the present time my quest was nothing more than to exist in a daily routine that turned me into a fully-fledged layabout. Tim's death had an effect on me which I didn't fully realize at the time. It left me empty and hard, trying to fill the void with anything that would help me forget that I could easily be lying under the cold ground in a country graveyard.

Your life stepped lightly out our hands.

I'd meet Mark in Slaten most mornings at around eleven-thirty, as he normally opened his eyes the moment the Temple opened its doors. I'd catch sight of him shuffling into view in his crumpled old grey suit, the racing form under his arm and a five o'clock shadow heavy on his bloodless face. We would sit in the pub and converse with the lunch crowd until they returned to work and left us alone playing snooker or discussing the afternoon's certainties at Newmarket and Exeter. I was never obsessive about horse racing and it was only Mark's fanaticism that stirred me to take any interest at all, faking what little knowledge I had and tossing him the occasional half-crown for a round robin. In this way I passed the days becoming increasingly lazy and more inclined to consider this lifestyle quite palatable. I also spent time in the company of Red Thomas who, like myself and Mark, had a distinct disinterest in work while enjoying any form of petty crime that might make him a few quid. With these two companions to share my labourless days you can imagine that my interests became extremely base; a sixteen-year-old whose influences were unhealthy, to say the least. During these months, however, I scored a resounding victory in the romantic sweepstakes.

There was a couple locally who could often be seen around town absolutely engrossed in each other. It seemed to me that they were a pair very much in love. Although his name escapes me, hers was Sally Bennington and I thought she was the most beautiful creature I'd ever seen. Benni, as she was known to me, was petite and designed with precision. Other than the obvious, what caused me to develop this mad crush on her was that she was several years my senior. This fact, coupled with her devotion to her boyfriend, only made my chance of landing her remote at best. When it happened it was as if I had dreamt it and, like a blow to the back of my skull, Benni entered my life, making my heart truly ache for the first time.

One night at the Temple I glanced up from my drink to see her standing across the room chatting with some friends. What struck me immediately was that she was on her own, the normal appendage being nowhere in sight. My heart began to pound uncontrollably and I was forced to lay my hand on my chest lest

157

the sounds of my desire be heard above the din. For all my exterior cockiness I was in fact painfully shy in my approach to girls, a trait occasionally working to my advantage in the long run. You can imagine my reaction when she walked over and attempted to strike up a conversation. My tongue became instantly knotted and it was all I could do to prevent my legs from buckling beneath me. Here was a real woman, one whom I thought was totally oblivious to my existence, standing before me staring into my eyes. To the best of my ability I attempted to remain calm and appear indifferent, which I found all but impossible, and as we danced I professed to the attraction I had felt for her from afar. She seemed genuinely touched by my sincere but schoolboyish approach and soon we were engrossed in conversation. This was the dawn of true love, and with Benni I embarked on a romance that was to teach me much about passion, frustration and pain.

Benni lived with her girlfriend in a small semi-detached behind the gasworks. The house was owned by the girl's mother, a flamboyant character who was for ever entertaining a steady flow of fancy men. I found the atmosphere in the house enjoyable, as there was always a friendly welcome and a drink to be had. Her friend Yvonne was a skinny Mod type who, along with Benni, was surprisingly hip for the area and, together with Yvonne's blowzy mother, made the place a casual and easy spot in which to relax. Benni was a spirited girl and enjoyed social life to the full. I got the feeling she had felt smothered in her prior relationship and was taking advantage of this new lease of life. We were continually in each other's arms, spending literally hours entwined in a smooching embrace in the alley beside her home. During the day she worked at the plastics factory and in the afternoon I met her by the gate and walked her home. Proud of my conquest, I paraded her before my friends like some prize poodle. They were suitably impressed and perhaps a little jealous, but did their best to contain it.

My lifestyle continued in this way until I was forced by my limited cash-flow to seek part-time employment for a few extra quid. While my father's financial aid was much appreciated, my tastes for the good life were running high and in order to maintain them it was necessary to attempt a little labour. I declined several offers from Red entailing money by illegal gain which, although I was far from being a saint, involved more risk than I wished to take. I had, however, unwittingly been his accomplice in one break-in. He'd told me he was staying with a friend in a flat above a furniture store in the High Street and that his friend had left for the weekend forgetting to leave Red the key. Totally believing this fabrication, I had stood and allowed him to clamber on to my shoulders as he forced the window and disappeared inside. While he was inside rifling the till I had innocently conversed with a bobby on night duty, never thinking for a minute that I was aiding Red's breaking and entering.

It was one weekend when the boys and I were over at Shannon's that opportunity knocked. Across from Shannon's home in Shelton was a broiler farm called Denholm Holdings. For those unaware of this rather depressing form of poultry farming, chickens raised as broilers are considered by many to be tastier than the free-range or battery product. This procedure is achieved by transporting day-old chicks straight from the hatchery to the broiler house, a large oblong building devoid of windows and constantly illuminated. Kept extremely warm, the birds live in comfort, sleeping on wood shavings and eating continually from feeders strung every few feet around the building. At first the chicks are kept in circular pens which are gradually widened as they grow, until ultimately they have a free run of the building. Their entire life is lived out in artificial light, and when they reach maturity trucks arrive in the middle of the night to transport them to your local freezer. For this job extra help is required to catch and crate them; and that was where I came in.

Years earlier I had done the same thing on my father's smaller enterprise, our family being dragged from our beds to help round up the dozing chickens, so if any experience was necessary, I could say I had it. It was dirty work and the dust kicked up by the catcher's feet stung my eyes and clung to my throat. The chickens reacted stubbornly to being manhandled, and made their feelings known by pecking and scratching my exposed hands and fingers. The idea was to sweep them up by their feet and carry them out, four in each hand. In time I became expert at this, adopting mask, goggles and gloves to protect me from the aforementioned dangers. It was gruelling work, to say the least, and the monotonous routine of returning to and from the truck was not for the faint of heart. They worked us all hard and paid us well, but no shirking was tolerated and in order to remain in the team it was necessary to toe the line. We were fit and strong due to the air we breathed, which gave us a distinct edge over the old boys present. My sterling efforts in catching and crating paid off, and after several of these evenings I was offered a full-time job on the farm. Realizing the necessity of paid employment, I accepted. After all this time I ended up where I'd started out, on the farm, the very place I'd sworn never to be. Hopefully my father saw the irony in this, considering he'd sold his farm after realizing that none of his sons wished to work on it. Aside from this simple twist of fate, my folks were relieved and I, once more employed, was resigned to the fact that this was to be my lot in life.

I began to rise again at cockcrow in order to cycle to the farm in Shelton. Initially I was given menial tasks, such as hosing slats, cleaning out the shavings and scrubbing the concrete floors, which were necessary in order to prepare for the new arrivals. They could be accepted only when the entire environment was totally sterile. Disease was rampant and one attack of fowl-pest could wipe out the entire stock, so the broiler houses were scrubbed until the floors were fit to eat off.

The owner was rarely around and the day-to-day running of the place was left in the hands of his foreman, Art Reardon. My first impression of Art was that he seemed a colourful character, full of jokes and stories and friendly enough to appear a reasonable boss. However, I found in time that this was not the case and that first impressions can often prove deceptive.

After a few weeks in Shelton, Art informed me that commencing on Monday we'd be moving to Denholm's sister site in Doramby, which was fine by me as it meant literally a ten-minute ride to work and precious extra time in bed. Art and his wife Thelma would live in the house on the property and he and I would be working the place together.

The Doramby site lay at the bottom of a long lane in the farthest corner of the village, far from the madding crowd. It stood alone, surrounded by acres of arable farmland, a target for the cruel winds of winter. There were three broiler houses along with several sheds and barns housing our equipment and feed, as well as an overabundance of enormous rats. In my spare time I sat on a pile of chicken crates blasting these monsters with a 4·10. Completely unstoppable, their numbers seemed to multiply instead of diminish, and with heroic idiocy they charged back and forth along the walls daring to be destroyed. Undaunted in death, these creatures seemed to cling to contempt even as they spun through the air, lifeless and full of lead. The days consisted of feeding and watering and watering and feeding, a monotonous cycle due to the birds' immense appetites. It was all they ever did and I imagine, in the same circumstances, I would have done the same. It wasn't exciting or rewarding work, but for the time being I was content and continued to think a little more variety lay just around the corner.

Mark was disappointed that I had rejoined the work force but did nothing to reinstate himself, preferring to continue sinking pints and staring at the racing form. Through these turbulent months, the one thing that had not changed was my relationship with Rick, Eddie and Steve. We were still a tight group whose unity was the mainstay of our sanity and with my return to work we were once more in harmony with each other. With what I thought was the worst behind me, we set out on a rejuvenated phase. I was relieved to have a steady wage, and the actual means by which I was earning it did nothing to depress me. It was cold hard cash with which I was able to date Benni in reasonable style. Together with the boys, or occasionally without them, Benni and I utilized the services of Shannon and Neil who were once more mobile. *En masse* we ventured far and wide, attending local dances and 'happening' pubs, or travelling to the ballrooms in Boston and Grimsby. It was a carefree time as I regained some of the old spirit dampened by my unemployment and Tim's death. The fact that my illusions were but dust in the wind was pushed to the back of my mind as, with a shovel of my own design, I dug myself into a neat little hole. If this evaluation chanced to cross my mind, I only went to greater lengths to convince myself that I was indeed happy in my cell.

We were no longer inclined to indulge in our previous tastes for crime sprees, tending to stick instead to basic bawdy drunken behaviour. The rebellious spirit was all but dead and we became caricatures of the small-town defeatists we had once despised. At least in our previous thievery and depravity we had borne forth a certain amount of imagination, no matter how twisted it might have been. Now we basically went out on the town and made fools of ourselves. Altercations were no longer dreamed up, they were dealt out, as our rambunctious behaviour lost its original naivety and charm. We were working and living hard, and on one particular evening in the spring of '67 an incident occurred which made me realize that where innocence ends, there begins violence.

There was still a great deal of resentment towards me and the boys by the local lads in Doramby. As far back as the arrival of Eddie, Rick and Steve at Doramby Youth Club they had felt insulted that I had chosen to befriend outsiders and desert the home camp. This, along with the fact that they had been left off the guest list at our White Rhino parties, hadn't helped matters. You would think that as we grew older rivalries and differences would have been forgotten, but in this case they simmered slowly for years until the two factions could not hold court in the same place. We made a point of not irritating each other by poaching territory, but on one occasion the Doramby contingent came to Slaten knowing full well that the Temple was our stronghold. We were in force on this particular night and also had in our company Paul Bundy, the tree-basher from the Rhino party. Paul was still intent on making an impression on us and ever on the look-out for trouble in which he might incorporate the use of his fists. By this time we had gathered around us an odd assortment of regulars who were appreciated for their muscle rather than their character. Little of this crossed my mind and I merely accepted each and every one of them as more power.

The Temple was packed to the rafters and after an hour or so's drinking someone informed us that the enemy was flaunting itself in the bar. Their most formidable member was a stocky kid by the name of Noël Gordon who particularly disliked Eddie, a feeling that was mutual. Fuelled by the evening's intake, we became increasingly irritated at this brazen act of hostility and by the time the pub was emptying out, the clans were gathering in the market place. There were taunts and threats thrown back and forth until it seemed inevitable that the outcome would be decided by Eddie and Noël. The two of them stared each other down and began pushing each other roughly, until finally the punches flew. Immediately a circle formed, as both sides eyed each other lest anyone try to intervene in this test of champions.

So far we had avoided an all-out brawl, but any slip could cause the entire group to explode. After a series of blows had been exchanged, drawing blood on both their faces, Eddie got the upper hand and soon his competition was staked out beneath him. It was not a pretty sight and, as the girls screamed with fright, Eddie laid waste to his opponent in a fit of fury. Seeing him administer such punishment was unsettling, and there was no doubt a blood-lust had taken over. Repeatedly he rammed Noël's face into the cobblestones until his friends felt it necessary to throw in the towel. With difficulty we dragged Eddie off Noël just as the police arrived. The incident had become ugly and seeing him transformed into a killing machine was frightening. The enemy picked up its defeated comrade and was reassembling him as the notebook appeared from the officer's top pocket. No one said a word and, with all due respect to our adversaries, they indicated that nothing serious had occurred and the whole affair was just a friendly wrestle. This gesture broke the barriers, as hands were shaken and amends made. It seems that in order to unite independent gangs it is often necessary to beat the living daylights out of each other first.

The officer was quite peeved that this fracas had caused such harmony and attempted to intimidate us by interrogation.

'Where are you from?'

'Spridillby, officer,' said Eddie.

'Where's that, boy?'

'Near where he lives,' Eddie answered, indicating me.

'And where do you live?' he snapped.

'Bramby,' I said.

'And where might that be?'

'Near Spridillby, sir,' I replied.

This copper was becoming extremely annoyed.

'Don't be funny, lad, where the hell is Bramby and Spridillby?'

At this point Noël interjected, 'Just down the road from me, sir.'

'Where the bloody hell is that?' he retaliated in exasperation.

'Doramby,' Noël said.

'How far away is that?' queried the confused fuzz.

'Just down the road from Bramby.'

The policeman was at the end of his tether at this point. 'I don't mean from there, you moron!'

Eddie jumped in. 'You mean from Spridillby?'

That did it! The officer exploded. 'No, dammit, from here!'

163

'Where's here?' I chimed in.

He threw up his arms. 'Market Slaten, and you know it, lad!'

In unison we lapsed into excited mumbling, repeating the town's name over and over with grave reverence. Realizing he was in the presence of major weirdness, the policeman compromised unwillingly, threatening to arrest us all unless we vacated the market place in the next five minutes. Intent on making a grand exit, we thanked him profusely, dropped to our knees and filed out of the market place in a dwarf-like conga line, singing, *'Heigh ho, heigh ho, it's off to work we go, with a knife and fork and a bellyful of pork, heigh ho, heigh ho . . .'*

The evening didn't end on this note and when we reached the car Paul, satiated with blood-lust, decided he wanted to make a scene. He placed his hand on my shoulder and began to harangue me with accusations that it was my doing he was not accepted into the inner sanctum of our group. I really wasn't in the mood for this and pushed his arm aside, attempting to ignore him, which only irritated him further. He shoved me hard against the side of the car, an equally annoying gesture that seemed to be the inevitable prelude to another fight. It was a child-like attitude for Paul to take and one from which he finally backed down when my friends naturally took my side in attempting to reason with stupidity. This was only one of many occasions when these silly feuds exploded into primitive acts, and it's not hard to see how redundant sometimes was the merry-go-round on which we rotated.

> *Saturday night's alright for fightin'*
> *Get a little action in . . .*

———————

With the improvement of my financial status due to long hours of overtime, my thoughts turned to buying a motorbike. A friend in Shelton called Chris Smith had a machine he wished to part with and I had my heart set on it. The only obstacle was my father's intense dislike of motorbikes, as he felt they were death-traps and not to be trusted. However, after much grovelling and desperate reasoning as to how it would be helpful in my job, he relented and allowed me to buy it. The following Saturday morning he drove me to Chris's to give it the parental once-over before purchase. It was a rather splendid bike indeed and even my dubious dad had to admit the maroon BSA Goldstar was a good buy. The transaction complete and the necessary papers having changed hands, my father drove off leaving Chris to explain the bike's finer points. Not very good at following instructions, I manoeuvred the thing home without taking it out of first gear.

I never did master my bike completely and only after several weeks did I learn the art of changing gear without it grinding with irritating regularity. I immediately rode over to Spridillby to show off my bike to the boys. Suitably impressed, they begged me to let them test her out themselves. I was not in favour of allowing this but found it impossible to refuse this request from my best friends. Rick and Steve managed admirably and whizzed up and down the road with expertise. It was only when Eddie mounted it that things went wrong. Eddie, you see, was left-handed and as he sped off up the road he mistook the back brake for the clutch. Instead of changing into second, he came to a screeching halt and was pitched forward into the air, landing several yards ahead of the machine. Adding insult to injury, I ran to my machine concerned for its well-being, leaving Eddie spread-eagled in the middle of the road. I was annoyed that he had allowed such a thing to happen and left him where he was, indicating that the extent of his injuries could never be sufficient to appease me.

Realizing I wasn't letting him near my bike again, Eddie bought one for himself a week later. It was not as impressive as mine, being several years older and about 100 ccs less; still, I was happy I now had a companion with whom to share the experience of motorbiking. Together we roared around, showing off with the absolute minimum of skill. It seemed we were all becoming mobile, as shortly thereafter Steve got a terrific deal on a little green Triumph Herald. Unfortunately it didn't prove to be that terrific and was for ever sitting on the Easts' front lawn with the bonnet open and Steve leaning inside hurling out various parts. We did get some use out of it and, after so many years of foot-slogging, hitch-hiking and conning lifts, it was nice to be independent at last. It came at a good time, as Shannon had recently taken up with Eddie's sister Diane and was by now at the besotted stage. Initially the feeling did not appear to be mutual, and Shannon was under a tremendous amount of pressure to secure her devotion. To make matters worse, Eddie's father, realizing that Shannon most definitely did not ride with the hunt, was against the whole thing from the outset.

Neil too was romantically involved, a fact we found remarkable, being unable to imagine any woman in her right mind wanting to brush lips with such an unattractive face. Obviously we were wrong, as the girl in question turned out to be quite pretty, even though she was prim, prudish and favoured a hairstyle that appeared to be constructed with scaffolding. She took an instant dislike to us, doing everything in her power to keep Neil free from our influence. This of course made us wish to be all the more visible, and whenever possible we went out of our way to be present, hovering around her hair, screaming orders for assembly and mimicking the sounds of power tools. As for my amorous self, Benni was my obsession but even this seemingly healthy relationship was suffering its first setback.

I was extremely keen to advance my sexual schooling, which in a nutshell meant I was desperate to lose my virginity. Benni was without a doubt going to be the one to show me how. She was older and, I imagined, a woman of experience, most definitely my best prospect so far. I was wrong, and after a month of courtship we were no further than the kissing stage which was indeed passionate, but any attempt by my roving hands was halted unceremoniously. I had achieved more than this with Daphne several years earlier, and not being able to grope this petite sexpot was frustrating, to say the least. Whenever sex was brought up she was on the defensive, changing the subject or explaining unconvincingly that only time could tell. Still, I was so in love that even this barrier was not enough to have me wander off in search of looser virtues. Aside from this setback, Benni was still an impressive sight on my arm and nothing was about to make me change my mind.

. . . and lovers leap off burning buildings.

Meanwhile, back on the farm, Art Reardon was beginning to show his true colours. It was becoming more apparent that, besides being a major bullshitter, Art was none too fond of hard work and one of those people who administered jobs that he was not prepared to do himself. Most days I did the bulk of the work,

166

running the place while he played hookey. I would rise around six-thirty and ride my bike through the sleeping village as, with idle hands, the first light of day dragged itself above the horizon. Behind drawn curtains the work force stirred in its slumber, their shadows illuminated as a harsh wattage shook them awake. Toy figures in slow motion, they acted out their morning ritual as I watched them wake like a living negative on a silent screen. The stillness inside was countered by a dawn chorus as the trees and hedgerows burst forth into bird song. The long dew-laden grass bustled with morning activity and, faced with the day's labour, I was forced to appreciate Mother Nature's machinery hard at work.

The long deserted lane leading to the farm took on an eerie appearance at this early hour, the mist rising from the fields like a spectral curtain hovering above the swaying crops. The air was chilled and stung my face with reviving efficiency, causing my eyes to fill with cold tears and my cheeks and nose to shine with a crimson glow. It was necessary to watch the road with an eagle eye, as the fog and mist hid the busy cross-traffic of rabbits on the run. This world with all its nature was a lonely planet and from the road the farm could have been the last place on earth, sitting cold and alone in a desolate space. I manoeuvred my bike with caution through this solitary landscape, my lunchbag slapping my thigh and my head bowed to the oncoming wind. Arriving at the farm, I stored my bike in the barn and began feeding, a task taking up most of the morning and one which was both methodical and repetitive. I was beginning to believe chickens were neither bright nor endearing; in fact, I found them idiotic creatures that deserved everything they got, and would boot my way through them, indifferent to their squawks of protest. Sleeping and eating seemed to be their lot in life and, considering their surroundings, I presumed they had little choice. Even their state of living and dying in artificial light did nothing to soften my feelings and I reared them with no sense of remorse.

Art would arrive some time after ten, clutching his morning coffee and examining my progress. He would check to see if the bins were full and that I was not short-changing my charges in order to finish early. I took offence at this but said nothing; it was bad enough that he rolled in just as I was finishing off. I had already been there for three solid hours, hefting sacks and cutting

167

my hands on the feeders as I shook them to spread out their miserable pellets. By the time he arrived I was in no mood for his suggested accusations and cornball jokes. Deeply in love with his own character he seemed determined to force it upon me whether I liked it or not. When feeding was complete, I had a quick cup of tea and set about some other task, which ranged from scrubbing down slats and feeding-bins to unloading deliveries and stacking chicken crates.

Between the departure of the birds and the delivery of new arrivals, we set to cleaning the houses and preparing for these shipments. For this we hired outside labour, as the job was too much for two men – or one man actually, for Art couldn't be considered any help. During this time he would stand around, hose in hand, conducting the proceedings with presumed efficiency while we broke our backs with scrubbing-brushes and stiff-bristled brooms. It was remarkable and quite clever how Art Reardon could make the most minimal task seem Herculean. I hate to give him credit, but it was done with such condescending efficiency that he actually made it seem he was bearing the brunt of our labour. If someone was spotted not scrubbing with enough broom-power, Art would rush over with a frazzled, 'Not like that, like this!', demonstrating briefly before thrusting the broom back to the exhausted worker. He was totally oblivious to the fact that this employee had been at it for hours while his demonstration had taken all of two minutes. He commanded in this fashion, with a little scrub here and a little brush there, for ever giving the impression that we were pit-ponies and he was the shire-horse. Even with all this to contend with I was not altogether unhappy and was making a reasonable wage, getting enough fresh air and, thanks to Art's continual absence, plenty of time to contemplate life. In a way I was my own boss and that in itself gave me some satisfaction, enough at least to let me imagine I might be happy in this situation indefinitely.

With our new-found mobility it was now possible to get here and there without relying too much on our other friends. Steve's Triumph was far from reliable but it did manage to transport us on many occasions without breaking down. Eddie and I had taken to riding our bikes into Market Slaten on weekday evenings for the pure pleasure of the ride and the reward of a pint or two. This was rather amusing, as Eddie's bike had nowhere near the power of mine and in order to allow him to keep up I had to remain in first gear. I used this situation to my advantage and rebuked him mercilessly on the pathetic capabilities of his machine. Holding back, I would allow Eddie to take the lead, lulling him into thinking he had found new speed. This caused him to become over-confident and then suddenly I would change up and zoom past him, leaving him cursing in my wake. At other times I sidled up next to him, rocking in my seat backwards and forwards, mimicking the way he encouraged his bike as if riding a stubborn mule. With his normal good nature, he took it all in his stride and joined in the joke, cracking an imaginary whip above his head, urging his steed to pick up speed. One night, however, after considerable consumption at the Temple, Eddie was to have the last laugh.

Exiting rather unsteadily at closing time, I found that my bike refused to start, forcing me to leave it behind and ride home on Eddie's pillion, a situation from which my friend obtained tremendous mileage in verbal revenge. It was a foggy night and visibility was not good. There was a persistent drizzle and the road was becoming slick due to the sharp drop in temperature as the late night descended. Our rather rocky state and the fact that Eddie had never carried a passenger before did not help matters either. None of these obstacles being sufficient to deter us, we set out for home, all going well until we left the main road and set upon the tiny lanes leading to our villages. Here the deception of the weather played tricks on us, dropping dense masses of mist one second only to lift them the next, forming a gauntlet of guesswork for our tired minds. Our attention to detail was slight as Eddie swerved to left and right, clipping the verge and zigzagging erratically. We tried to alleviate these hazards by singing loudly and letting the cold night air fill our lungs and slap us rudely around the cheeks. All of a sudden we hit a dense patch of fog and for a frozen moment in time we travelled in an unidentifiable limbo. As quickly as it had come it was gone, leaving us speeding without hope into a sharp S-bend. Eddie applied his brakes but the ice beneath our wheels refused to acknowledge them, sending the bike into a spin. I was ejected gracelessly, crashing to the surface of the road and sliding along face-down for what seemed an eternity until I came to rest about fifty yards ahead.

Before I could take stock of the situation, I heard the horrible sound of approaching metal and, looking up in amazement, I saw Eddie's bike shoot past me in a shower of sparks. Man and machine were well and truly separated, bike ahead, me in the middle and Eddie somewhere behind. Coming to my senses, I heard his voice hanging on the wind like a desperate sailor clinging to a sinking ship, when all of a sudden he appeared through the mist, limping towards me and calling my name as if I were the last person on earth. When he saw me, there was obvious relief in his eyes and I could tell he was glad to find me alive. It was plain to see the accident had shaken him badly, and I began to look at my friend in a new light. Not that Eddie was insensitive, he was just always wary of showing an over-abundance of emotion lest it diffuse his roguish exterior. Even in my state of minor mutilation, it was gratifying to see him show his true feelings for a fallen comrade. I imagine my death on his conscience would have been unbearable; after all, if he had eliminated me, who would have cruised in tandem with him, making light of his chimp-like expertise?

. . . and it's good old country comfort in my bones.

Working daily in such isolation gave me hours to mull over life in general, as well as a renewed appreciation of my surroundings, reintroducing my memory to a simpler time. In my pursuit of manhood I had lost touch with much of my heritage, and sitting here now in a wilderness of raw nature I was once again able to understand why as a child I had been so happy. Not that I wished to remain rooted like some hardy perennial, only that I might once more come to terms with this wonderland, possibly finding an answer to what caused the endless aching in my heart. I was no doubt confused, constantly changing my point of view. I was both settled and unsettled, accepting my destiny one minute and refusing it the next. Here, alone on a cloud of country ideology, I was able to take a firmer grasp simply by watching the flight of migratory birds or the industrious action of bees. Nature seemed so resilient, never giving up, no matter what the elements threw at it – a code worth living by.

Perched on an upturned crate with my lunch on my lap, I surveyed the barren landscape. This county called Lincolnshire with its flat and arable fields, tended with vigorous repetition by the proud and tireless farmer, was a paradox of values. From where I sat I could see him in his cab dragging the rich brown earth and breaking it beneath disc and harrow. Clouds of seagulls circled above, shrieking in unison, as the wind carried on its drifting voice the smell of dampened soil. Dotted unevenly in this stark setting were hardy clumps of rough copse. Keeping company with these coarse nests stood the stooped frames of weather-beaten trees, aching like rheumatic pensioners hammered by the callous climate. For all its harsh appearance, it was hard not to perceive a wild beauty at work beneath the surface. Like a horse unridden and free of reins, the land was prepared to be tamed but never to lose its independence. The barns and buildings of the farm were a rich haven in the wild, a huge nest in a vast branch of the land. They were a refuge for every rodent, bird, beast and insect for miles around, and in the roofs and under the gutterings swallows and martins constructed elaborate fortifications against the cold. With mud and twigs they cemented their dwellings like true craftsmen, creating warm and safe orbs in which to raise their young. On closer detection in the early spring, it was possible to see bobbing heads mouthing at the air without sound, their blind and swollen eyes willing the return of mother and lunch.

Resilient too was the vegetation battling the elements out here along with each and every thing. It rose proudly from the ground, springing at random through the fading snow from the surrounding wasteground and manure heaps at the top of the farm. Nightshade and forget-me-nots struck a sharp contrast in the rocky earth and on the pungent tips, trooping their colours in the breeze like tiny battalions of floral heraldry. Farther into the fields and along the damp ditchline, the yellow trails of ragwort stretched with almost endless repetition. Dotted here and there clumps of fleabane and calvesfoot broke up their dominance, causing soft patches of colour conflicting with the yellow river of pollen. Seeing such common splendour before my eyes caused me to reflect on the country practices that as children we milked from the simplest flower. Sucking nectar from the cowslip or checking each other under the chin with a buttercup were just a

171

few of our pursuits in the long grass of summer where life was a ripple on the pool of infancy. Recapturing innocence, I placed between my palms a blade of thick green grass and blew, emitting a sharp high-pitched cry causing a pheasant to break from cover in startled panic. Considering my choices at the time, this certainly beat sitting on a bench inhaling carbon monoxide on Lindum Hill. There was little doubt that here in the wilderness was a country heart that could settle only for the best of both worlds.

Twelve

Spring progressed at a languid pace and my frustration with Benni's unwillingness to dispense sexual favours began to wear me a little thin. I found myself becoming more irritable although I refused to admit I was anything less than deeply in lust. It was also becoming glaringly obvious that she was not the knowledgeable older woman I took her for, and at times acted as if she were several years younger than the average fourth-former. I didn't like to admit these faults to myself, normally turning a blind eye when she acted childishly, but it was when we went to see the Small Faces at Boston Gliderdrome that I began to see my girlfriend in a different light. We were swaying with the crowd to the music when all of a sudden she totally lost her head and began scrambling through the crowd to the front of the stage, screaming like a giddy schoolgirl. I was both dumbstruck with embarrassment and annoyed at the same time. How could this tiny delight with whom I was desperately in love insult me by falling apart at the sight of some pimply-faced emaciated Mod? The more I thought about it the more I fumed, until my rage propelled me through the crowd to where she stood clinging like a sex-starved limpet to the edge of the stage. Grabbing her arm and hurling her round, I demanded she cease this unladylike behaviour and return to the bar with me before I did something I might regret. Obviously unimpressed by my assertion of masculinity, she mouthed something obscene, which I fortunately could not make out in the decibel storm surrounding us. That was it! I grabbed and dragged and she in return slapped and scratched, as a bewildered Steve Marriott peered down at us through a curtain of hair. My immediate reaction to him was a childish salute of two

173

fingers, a jealous response caused by his ability to evoke such animal instincts from a girl I could not coax beyond a lip-lock.

It was the beginning of an erosion in our relationship, and as we rode home in silence the atmosphere in the car dropped below freezing-point. On reflection it is amusing but at the time was extremely painful, as I was both infatuated and in love, although deep inside we were rotating in a vicious circle. Youthful sexual frustration was building a barrier between us and the rift in our thinking was causing an unhealthy pattern to exist. We spent hours alone in passionate embrace rolling around on the sofa or on her bed with nothing of an exploratory nature ever taking place, until in despair I threw up my arms, swung my legs over the edge of the bed and buried my face in my hands. Never wishing to get involved with anything more than surface emotions, Benni stalked out of the room, straightening her clothes and pouting. Things became more and more intolerable until I found myself once again seeking solace in the company of my friends.

By now we were spending Monday nights at a pub on the outskirts of Lincoln called the Wild Goose, one of the few places that could be relied upon for a good time on this normally dull day of the week. We usually pooled our resources for this one, as most of us were out of pocket after the weekend. We regarded the girls from Lincoln as up-market but got the distinct feeling they looked upon us as slightly plebeian. If the truth be known it was only their big city residence that gave them credibility. Still light years from Carnaby Street and the Kings Road, it was the wide variety that intrigued us and there were several who became favourites within our eyes but not within our arms. In time we became better acquainted, following them with regularity to hipper pubs such as the Pied Piper and the Swan, fully intent on conquering these damsels. One night, however, my pangs of guilt got the better of me, and leaving the boys in Lincoln I headed back to Slaten fully intent on a show-down with Benni. It was time we laid our cards on the table and if it meant cornering her in order to do it, so be it.

Arriving just as the pubs were emptying, I turned the corner into Union Street to see her walking towards me hand in hand with Chris Smith, the boy from whom I had bought my motorbike. My initial feeling was one of utter disbelief and I must

174

have looked rather stupid standing there with my mouth open, my body numbed by shock. Their reaction was much the same, and in this state of suspended animation Chris had the good sense to slip off and leave us to it. Warm tears filled my eyes and I turned to the wall, a gesture I hoped she would translate as disgust and not weakness. I did not wish it to be known that my sentimentality ran to such emotion, but nothing I could do would stem the flow. What the hell was this feeling? It wasn't supposed to happen like this; it never had before – I had always maintained a somewhat cavalier attitude. Then it struck me. It had never been this way round, I had never been the one deceived or cast off. In the past I had either called it a day or time had inevitably worn out the interest of both parties. Benni was speechless, as there was little to say and any humble apologies on her behalf were blurted out inaudibly as she pushed past me with her head down. For my part, I hurled some inane remark her way, as in my grief all I saw was a two-timing Jezebel who had struck a violent blow to my male pride.

As she disappeared into the late-night mist beyond the orange glow of the street lamp, I turned and rammed my fist into the wall with all my strength. The only pain I felt was in my heart – nothing as simple as a crushed hand could compare with such irreparable damage. As I sat there on the curb cradling my battered fingers, three pairs of legs appeared like an apparition before me and I looked up through tear-stained eyes into the sympathetic faces of my best friends. Apparently they had been aware of Benni's betrayal and, learning that I was intent on returning to Slaten, had followed me, fully suspecting I might be in need of emotional support. They turned a blind eye to my tears, having the decency to regard them as the effects of the damp evening weather. We knew better than to fall back on sentiment, feeling it inappropriate. The mere fact that we remained together in strength when one of us felt weak was enough to make our troubles bearable.

I refused a ride home, preferring to walk the seven miles even though the night was taking a turn for the worse. A thick blanket of fog was falling, bringing the light drizzle and clutching damp that is so characteristic of the north. Although I argued strongly against it, the boys were determined to opt out of their lift and join me. That night we reverted to our old ways and walked. The first miles were made in silence, each of us deep in our own thoughts, mine – as you might guess – of a reflective nature. Thinking back on the night's events I couldn't help feeling hurt, more so now that my battered hand was beginning to bruise and throb painfully. With all this playing on my heart-strings, it was not hard to see why the break had happened. It was inevitable in the lie we were both living that it was only a matter of time before one of us saw the truth. As the miles disappeared behind us a gentle breeze sprang up, forcing the clouds back across the heavens until the night sky was filled with stars and a full moon lit our way. Rick looked into the sky and remarked that there appeared to be a change in the weather, as I looked into my heart and prayed for a change in my life.

For the wide-eyed and laughing
Passed like a season
Erasing a passion to sin.

I was working harder than ever now and in May something occurred which caused me to put in continual overtime, pushing my endurance to the limit and resulting in an ultimate confrontation with Art Reardon. The farm was hit by a devastating outbreak of fowl-pest, which depleted our stock and caused panic in the community. It seemed that everywhere you turned farmers were suffering the most staggering losses. Aside from the fowl-pest, dairy herds up and down the country were in the grip of the worst outbreak of foot-and-mouth in history. In 1967 and 1968 alone over 400,000 beasts had to be slaughtered in order to halt its spread. What it must have been like for these poor men, to stand by helplessly as their prize herds were crippled with disease and destroyed, is unimaginable. For us the reality resulted in panic as we battened down the hatches and sealed ourselves in, in order to quell the plague.

Literally thousands of gallons of disinfectant were hosed, thrown and scrubbed into every nook and cranny that might harbour any lurking germs. We wore masks and rubber gloves at all times and were constantly stepping into troughs of disinfectant before entering or exiting the buildings. My every waking hour was spent keeping up with the constant flow of death as I waded in among the terrified birds, plucking out the dead like some corpse-collector from the Middle Ages. These I would load on to the back of a flatbed truck, which I would drive up to a large incinerator on the edge of the farm where I would shovel the carcasses into the flames with a pitchfork. The build-up of bodies was so rapid that it would be days before I would reach the bottom of the pile. The flames could not consume them fast enough and by the time I got to them they were green and fetid and crawling with maggots. Standing in the howling north wind shovelling death into the roaring fire was an all-time low, as the stench of charred flesh permeated even the thick gauze of my mask and caused me to gag much of the time. Naturally Art came nowhere near my Hades on earth, preferring to stay as far away from the inferno as possible. With all this going on and me at my wits' end, he still expected me to feed the living regularly and on time. I was nauseated by the fumes, sickened by the sight of dead chickens impaled on my pitchfork and fed up to the teeth with Art Reardon.

The final straw came on my birthday which happened to fall on a Sunday. With the outbreak of fowl-pest I had been working seven days a week and felt I was entitled to the day off. No deal. Art expected me in at the crack of dawn and made no bones about the outcome should I refuse. I wasn't prepared for a Mexican stand-off and agreed, on condition that once I had completed the feeding I would be free to go. That day I arrived at six and began the feed. Art turned up around ten with his 'I've been up since the crack of dawn' approach and immediately began sticking his nose into the feed bins with suspicion. Only today he made the mistake of berating me for cutting corners and not doing my job. I was in no mood to be labelled a liar, especially by someone who made a profession of it, and in no uncertain terms I told him so. The fur flew and my bottled hate was unleashed in a torrent of truths. All this obviously hit home, and as I strode from the building entirely satisfied with my performance he stood behind me spluttering my dismissal. I felt refreshed and free as I rode home, content in the knowledge that without my muscle he would no doubt fall to pieces, a victim of his own devices. It would take him a while to find a replacement, and in the meantime he would be forced to take the bull by the horns. Hopefully the bull would prove too much for him, trampling him in his lies and tossing him into the chicken shit.

177

Well, here I was seventeen years old and out of work again. I sat back in an armchair and stared at my parents. What was to be done? Once more their wayward son had seen fit to pull the plug on his employment. My father shrugged his shoulders and my mother let out a gentle sigh as she laid the table. Still, they chose not to chastize me and, while they were concerned, they whole-heartedly agreed with what I had done, fully supporting my mutiny. While waiting for lunch I flicked aimlessly through the pages of a music magazine, and as they fell through my fingers another world unfolded before my eyes – a world that had retained permanent residence in my mind ever since I'd heard Lonnie Donegan sing 'The Rock Island Line' on a scratchy seventy-eight many years before. Only now it seemed to be exploding into a new era of sight and sound, modern technology making so much more possible, as new ideas from inventive minds turned the record business upside-down.

In London and on the west coast of America the strict formulas of modern song-writing were being broken by the radical genius of men such as John Lennon and Brian Wilson. 'Sergeant Pepper' had been released and overshadowed all that had gone before, opening the floodgates to a torrent of imitators, none even coming close to surpassing the imagination of its perpetrators. In California bands such as Buffalo Springfield and the Byrds were blending together the roots of ethnic country with the vitality of modern rock, fusing it into a stirring magical sound. In San Francisco the ever-increasing influence of the drug culture reared a series of prolific groups such as the Grateful Dead and Jefferson Airplane. Everywhere you turned there was music in the streets, a backlash no doubt due to the violence in south-east Asia and on the banks of the Jordan River. Every day new cults and fashions were paraded before the media. The flower children with their idyllic principles sprang up at an alarming rate from Battersea to Haight-Ashbury. It mattered not in the least whether one's tastes were for beads and bells or marijuana and granny glasses. The backbone was the music pulsing like a trembling hand on the shoulders of a generation bent on revolution, only their war was one of gentle combat and music was their sword. It was a fanciful time and this spirit was echoed in the lyrical content of contemporary songs.

Bob Dylan had become a law unto himself, proving it was

178

possible to encase lengthy poetic pieces in strong melody – a trademark overstepping the boundaries of modern commercialism. Until now the simple single had been just that, but with 'Strawberry Fields' a major milestone was once more laid by Beatle magic. As I scanned my paper that very day, the ultimate example of this new trend was sitting at the top of the charts. Procol Harum's brilliant hymn-like anthem 'A Whiter Shade of Pale' broke all the traditional ingredients respected in a hit single and sat atop the charts beckoning all budding poets to take their verse and let it rock. I hadn't dabbled in any scribbling of late, but all this fresh energy encouraged me to put pen to paper once more. I spent the next few weeks crouched over a notebook, churning out reams of pretentious carbon copies of what was currently popular. Being jobless and loveless gave me fair cause to create, no matter how bad the end result. If nothing else I was at least returning in part to the ideals I had once gained from a well-read past.

Almost two months later, in July, I was scanning my weekly *New Musical Express* when I chanced upon an advertisement that caught my eye. It pertained to a record company called Liberty which was breaking away to go independent from EMI, the country's largest record distributor. In essence what they needed were the seeds with which to grow themselves a roster of artists, writers and production staff. I was immediately interested; here at least was a chance, no matter how slight. The problem I faced was that I had no musical ability, and without melodic accompaniment how could I be classed as a songwriter? Still, it was worth a shot. Maybe somewhere in their organization somebody might see something in my work worth pursuing. Somewhere there might be a melody missing words or some tin-pan-alley tunesmith struggling for the correct phrase to turn his tune to gold. After mulling over the reality behind my thinking, I decided it was worth it, for I had everything to gain and nothing to lose.

I've finally decided my future lies
beyond the yellow brick road.

I sat down and composed what I thought to be a bright and forceful letter, sealing it up in an envelope along with a selection of my work. In actual fact it was nothing more than pompous drivel accompanied by several sheets of abstract poetry reeking of verbosity. However, before I mailed it I got cold feet and stuck it on the mantelpiece behind the clock where it sat gathering dust for several weeks. Doubtless I felt I was taking liberties with Liberty, and my confidence was shaken as I pictured hordes of office girls gathered around my letter howling with laughter at the juvenile ramblings of a country bumpkin. While the letter stayed behind the clock, I strayed on the town and informed the boys of my plans to hit the big city. They were sceptical of my boasts but humoured me none the less. If I chose to think aloud, making my pipe-dreams public, then that was okay with them. I had after all just lost my job, and the aftershock had thrown me into an emotional dream where I countered misery with escapism. The more I dwelled in this fantasy, the more convinced I became that it was foolish to believe anything could come of it – until I looked up one day and noticed the envelope had gone. In a panic I made inquiries, discovering that my mother had posted it thinking I had forgotten to mail it previously. Her innocent gesture both saved and changed my life.

A week later I received an encouraging reply from a Raymond Williams who had found my work intriguing but, as I guessed, was unsure how to approach lyrics without music. The letter, however, requested that if I was going to be in the London area in the near future, I should pop in and have a word with them. The thing that most impressed me was the fact that they took me for the type who might 'pop into' London at any time! I wrote back post-haste saying I just happened to be planning such a trip and when would it be possible to make an appointment? As an afterthought I confronted my parents with this information and, as in everything else I'd ever done, they looked upon it as one more chance to shear the black sheep of his fleece. My dad got on the phone to his brother in Putney and it was arranged that for a small weekly fee I could stay in one of their extra bedrooms. Now that most of their boys were scattered around the globe in various occupations, the house was fairly quiet and my presence was not likely to be an inconvenience as my auntie, to whom I was very close, had promised to watch out for my well-being. So it was all set that the following week I would move to London to seek my fortune in the true spirit of Dick Whittington.

That evening I walked alone in the fields and up the cow-path leading across the Todmoor to the Angel Tree. Seated on the stump of that long-gone giant, I stared down on my tiny village. In comparison with where I was bound it was an insignificant blot, barely warranting a mention on a map of the county. For almost ten years, though, this secluded spot off the beaten track had been a port in the storm during my most turbulent times. Its grey-stone cottages and red-bricked council houses were as familiar to me as the back of my hand and its low Roman walls, moss-covered and ravaged by time, had always led me home in a straight line. As a large red sun sank slowly on the horizon, Bramby became a silhouette, its irregular buildings rising and falling like a tiny cut-out constructed by childish hands. As the twilight descended, the squat tower of the parish church stooped slightly and rose from the ground like a great square tooth. Seeing it reminded me of my expedition to the summit so many summers gone, and I smiled easily recalling how much larger it had loomed back then. The last rays of the sun picked out the white lime gravestones sprouting through the unkept grass surrounding the church, and I could make out the tiny figure of the vicar standing at the door welcoming the congregation to evensong.

All was silent now but for the sound of insects. Flies buzzed lazily above cow-patties and in the clover close by a grasshopper struck up its mating call. Several bees, like light aircraft in formation, flew over the field winging back to the hive with the last pollen of the day. There was little doubt I had grown, but here in the fields I had once conquered with sword and sorcery nothing had changed. I had charged down these slopes and forded these streams, ridden imaginary horses through the woods and slain dragons in the tall corn. The dragons were gone but the corn still grew. My horse had been unridden for years, but if I listened closely I could still hear his hoofbeats on the wind. It was with all these things that I must now reconvene. If I reintroduced my imagination to the fables lost with the years, it might be possible to find in them words that warranted my success in the outside world. If I was to succeed, it was necessary to throw a line into the past and rope rhyme from the ghost of my grandfather.

I read books and draw life from the eye . . .

181

When my friends saw that my plans to move down south were genuine, they decided a party was in order – and where better to celebrate than in my second home? The Temple Arms was packed on the night prior to my departure, and although most of those present thought I would be back on the next train they went out of their way to pitch in and wish me well. Few of them understood what it was I was undertaking, and even those who did were sceptical about my qualifications. These people knew me only as a good-natured wide-boy, who with his gang of mates had become a permanent fixture in the ruling class for years. None of them had the slightest knowledge of my literary leanings, and had they known of my affection for the pen might have ostracized me years ago. What I was attempting was light years from their comprehension. To them pop stars were tin gods with gossamer wings smiling at them from glossy magazines and TV screens, whose reality was dubious and with whom actual contact was impossible for the northern man many miles from the new nirvana. I understood their feelings, for it was hard enough for me to accept the idea myself. I sat there in the corner of the lounge looking into their faces, all the more determined to succeed. No longer could I stand the prospect of being chained and bound to a life preordained before it happened. It was now or never. If I made it happen it would be glorious, and if I failed I would admit defeat and return. 'Better to have loved and lost . . .'

. . . all my life is drawings from the eye.

There was a low mist on the land and the sun seemed reluctant to make an appearance as I walked towards the car clutching a small brown suitcase. My head throbbed with dull pain from the previous evening's revelry, and it took all my strength to muster a confident smile for the benefit of my mother as she stood waving me off from the back step. It would have been easy to call it off at the last minute and return to a warm bed, so simple to say I had changed my mind and join my friends later for a leisurely pint before an open fire. I could even renege on my artistic will and return to the want ads for casual labour in a one-dimensional life. It was this final image and the thought of a pregnant wife and screaming kids drooling and puking in my lap that did it. I ran towards the car, threw my case in the boot and looked back only to gaze briefly at my mother with love.

The seven-thirty train from St Mark's to King's Cross was prompt and I clambered aboard, hesitant at how to bid my father farewell. This man who had made it all possible remained cautious and calm to the end. He handed me my suitcase and we nodded to each other with understanding written on our faces. All of a sudden, as if prompted by the conductor's whistle, I leaned forward and kissed him hard on the cheek. His eyes glistened momentarily as he turned away and was gone. Sitting back in my seat I stared through the grubby window at his disappearing car as the train pulled out of the station. There was nothing left for me now but to put my hopes in the hands of God, a gentleman with whom I had little to do of late. If indeed he was to help me, then I had better put some time aside to get reacquainted.

The countryside slipped by like stolen moments of my life, as we swept through fields of yellow mustard and acres of golden corn, along green rivers and snaking streams rising at the side to lush and thorny heaths. On a skinny towpath a couple walked their dog, throwing it sticks to retrieve, while brickworks and kilns belched out smoke in the distance behind them. Abandoned stations overgrown with ivy and wild roses flashed by, their old white signal boxes creaking in the wake of our speed. Leaving the land of D. H. Lawrence and Tennyson, we sped through Cambridge and closer to Conan Doyle and Dickens. My reflection in the grease-stained window smiled back at me as the rhythmic clickety-clack of the wheels lulled me into a sense of well-being, reminding me of a childhood story.

Like 'The Little Engine That Could' I was undertaking a challenge that would require all my strength, and as I fell asleep under the spell of the wheels, the words it repeated filled my ears and it was all I heard. *'I think I can, I think I can, I think I can . . .'*

Acknowledgments

The author and publishers are grateful to the following for permission to reproduce copyright material:

Big Pig Music, Ltd: p.51 'Cage the Songbird' by Elton John and Bernie Taupin © 1976 Big Pig Music, Ltd; p.66 'Captain Fantastic and the Brown Dirt Cowboy' by Elton John and Bernie Taupin © 1975 Big Pig Music, Ltd; p.109 'The Fox' by Elton John and Bernie Taupin © 1981 Big Pig Music, Ltd; p.115 'Writing' by Elton John and Bernie Taupin © 1975 Big Pig Music, Ltd; p.130 'Bitch is Back' by Elton John and Bernie Taupin © 1974 Big Pig Music, Ltd; p.147 'One More Arrow' by Elton John and Bernie Taupin © 1983 Big Pig Music, Ltd; p.149 'Sad Songs' by Elton John and Bernie Taupin © 1984 Big Pig Music, Ltd; p.157 'Cold Highway' by Bernie Taupin © 1974 Big Pig Music, Ltd; p.166 'Burning Buildings' by Elton John and Bernie Taupin © 1984 Big Pig Music, Ltd; p.176 'The Wide Eyed and Laughing' by Elton John and Bernie Taupin © 1976 Big Pig Music, Ltd.

All rights controlled and administered by Big Pig Music, Ltd. All rights reserved. International copyright secured. Copyright used by permission of Big Pig Music, Ltd.

Chappell & Co./Chappell Music, Ltd: p.93 'Catch the Wind' by Donovan Leitch © 1965 Chappell & Co. All rights reserved. Used by permission; p.164 'Heigh Ho' by Frank Churchill and Larry Morey © 1938 Bourne, Inc. USA. Rights for the United Kingdom and Commonwealth excluding Canada – Chappell Music, Ltd, London. Used by permission.

Dwarf Music: p.110 'Most Likely You Go Your Way (I'll Go Mine)' by